ADVAN
Renewing Ind...

"This book highlights age-old problems, including disastrous federal policies that undermined tribal governments and handicapped tribal economies, and it also highlights innovative, tribally developed solutions to these problems, demonstrating that the path to reinvigorating tribal markets and economies runs through tribal self-governance. The book is also a good reminder that tribes exercising sovereignty and self-governance have a responsibility to create stable economic regimes to attract investment to reservations."

—**Kevin Washburn**, former assistant secretary for Indian affairs, US Department of the Interior

"Sharing our jurisdictional innovations is the only way we will creatively destroy colonialism and renew our economies. This book is full of practical examples that tribes have developed and advanced to support more sustainable economies and communities. This should be part of the applied economics curriculum in every tribal college."

—**Manny Jules**, former chief of the Kamloops Band of Canadian First Nations and chief commissioner of the First Nations Tax Commission

"Drawing on historical, legal, and business data, Anderson and Ratté provide fresh insights into precontact and colonial American Indian tribal economies, unique cultural landscapes in Indian Country, and practical pathways forward based on contemporary tribal success stories. This important study is a must-read for tribal governments and citizens alike who are looking to establish economic sovereignty and entrepreneurial self-sufficiency."

—**David Sickey**, Coushatta Tribe of Louisiana chairman and council member, 2003–21, and founder and CEO of Sickey Global Strategies

RENEWING INDIGENOUS ECONOMIES

The Hoover Institution gratefully acknowledges the following individuals and foundations for their significant support of the HOOVER PROJECT ON RENEWING INDIGENOUS ECONOMIES *and this publication:*

The Fred Maytag Family Foundation

Koret Foundation

Gianforte Family Foundation

Searle Freedom Trust

John and Jean De Nault Family

Beach Foundation

Atlas Network

Liberty to Grow Foundation

RENEWING INDIGENOUS ECONOMIES

TERRY L. ANDERSON
KATHY RATTÉ

HOOVER INSTITUTION PRESS
STANFORD UNIVERSITY | STANFORD, CALIFORNIA

hoover.org

Hoover Institution Press Publication No. 723

Hoover Institution at Leland Stanford Junior University,
Stanford, California 94305-6003

First printing 2022
28 27 26 25 24 23 22   7 6 5 4 3 2 1

Manufactured in the United States of America
Printed on acid-free, archival-quality paper

Library of Congress Cataloging-in-Publication Data
Names: Anderson, Terry L. (Terry Lee), 1946- author. | Ratté, Kathy, author.
Title: Renewing indigenous economies / Terry L. Anderson, Kathy Ratté.
Other titles: Hoover Institution Press publication ; 723.
Description: Stanford, California : Hoover Institution Press, Stanford University 2022.
  | Series: Hoover Institution Press publication ; no. 723 | Includes bibliographical
  references and index. | Summary: "Describes how Native American tribes can
  strengthen sovereignty, property rights, and the rule of law to better integrate
  into modern economies, building a foundation for self-sufficiency and restoring
  dignity"—Provided by publisher.
Identifiers: LCCN 2021053813 (print) | LCCN 2021053814 (ebook) |
  ISBN 9780817924959 (paperback) | ISBN 9780817924966 (epub) |
  ISBN 9780817924980 (pdf)
Subjects: LCSH: Indians of North America—Economic conditions. |
  Indian reservations—Economic aspects—United States. | Indians of
  North America—Land tenure. | Right of property—United States. | Indians
  of North America—Government relations.
Classification: LCC E98.E2 A525 2022 (print) | LCC E98.E2 (ebook) |
  DDC 970.004/97—dc23/eng/20211106
LC record available at https://lccn.loc.gov/2021053813
LC ebook record available at https://lccn.loc.gov/2021053814

Our ancestors,
shining through the
north star and the
southern cross,
have connected us to
work together and
learn from one another.

We share the Pacific Ocean.
We share the wealth,
life and imagination the
ocean has brought to our
lands. The waka and the
canoe, symbols of teamwork
and determination,
have brought us to new and
different places.

—MANNY JULES

CONTENTS

FOREWORD

Despite differences in language, culture, and philosophies, Indigenous nations and communities want what other societies around the globe want: the ability to thrive and accomplish societal goals on a strong economic footing. These goals often encompass maintaining healthy food systems and sustainable housing and lifeways, with leisure time to enjoy families, songs, and the arts. For millennia, Indigenous nations and communities had just that.

When Europeans arrived in the "new world," they did not find struggling people with no agriculture, no trade and commerce, and no rule of law. The opposite is true. Europeans encountered a diversity of Indigenous societies who engaged in commerce with one another. This economic structure was not just a means to accomplish self-sufficiency; it was also a choice to maximize quality of life, on each community's unique terms.

Indigenous societies were governed by their own laws, customs, norms, and regulations, many of which provided protections for individual liberties that were unimaginable (and perhaps unrecognizable) to Europeans of the time. These often included safety nets against gendered violence, elaborate land tenure systems, and systems of conflict resolution with internal and external legitimacy.

Over the last few centuries, the impact of ongoing colonization shifted most Indigenous nations and communities from a focus on growing and thriving to a reactive and requisite survival mode. At the most base level, a primary focus on survival means protecting persons and territories from external assault. A secondary but equally important survival mode is to sustain and protect languages, religions, cultural knowledge, and Indigenous identity.

One aspect of that survival mode has been wielding the energy to push back against invisibility in a world that either does not or cannot see modern Indigenous people and their nations as they are and as they have been. Part of transitioning back to thriving communities is asserting the power to reclaim the narrative of past and present. The stories of Indigenous success, and the potential for future success, are far more powerful (and accurate) than the tired colonial portrayals of all things Indigenous.

The pages ahead in this book do some heavy lifting for setting the historical record straight when it comes to Indigenous economies and the potential for a return to sustainable, *thriving* economies. These economies will be conceived by and executed by Indigenous actors, as they have been in the past and present and will be in the future.

There is currently a revival underway in Indian country—in a diversity of places, in a diversity of ways, and at varying speeds of recovery. Where Indigenous nations are showing signs of an economic recovery, this is happening in spite of ongoing colonization, not because of it. Barriers such as dual taxation, a lack of recognition of tribal autonomy, and a series of other internal and external constraints make it more difficult to achieve a diverse economy with a healthy mix of tribally owned businesses and private-sector Indigenous business owners.

How did we get to this place? How did these challenges become normalized and acceptable and repetitive? What are the solutions? How do we empower Indigenous leaders and individuals to return to a path of Indigenous entrepreneurship as uniquely defined for, and by, each community?

Each of these questions warrants significant attention, critical treatment, and investment of time and resources. As this book highlights, the answers likely start with the dismantling of many things: stale narratives, colonially imposed structures, lack of Indigenous autonomy and infrastructure, and internal challenges that cannot be wholly addressed by local governmental action. The solutions cannot be accomplished overnight or in a vacuum that provides one monolithic approach. Wrapped up in any solution must be a deep understanding that Indian country is as diverse today as it was at the time of European contact. Solutions and progress will vary for each community. Just as each community has its own language, culture, and history, each also experiences colonization in a different way, carrying into the future a unique political and legal reality.

If there is an endgame, it is a simple one with an increasingly complex strategy. It is a return of thriving Indigenous economies, where each community uniquely defines the path of restoration and the contours of what it means to succeed. The pages ahead confront popular stereotypes of the past and present and share thoughtful examples that highlight the challenges that may unnecessarily cloud the path of an Indigenous economic renaissance.

Stacy Leeds
*Foundation Professor
of Law and Leadership,
Arizona State University
Former Justice,
Cherokee Nation
Supreme Court*

ACKNOWLEDGMENTS

This book borrows heavily, with permission, from the Tulo Centre for Indigenous Economics book, *Building a First Nation Investment Climate* (Kamloops, BC: Tulo Centre of Indigenous Economics, 2014, https://www.tulo.ca). That volume provided a template on which we could "Americanize" the examples, laws, and political climate. The Tulo Centre has tested its volume with tribal leaders and students for several years, giving us confidence in the success of its book. We thank André Le Dressay, a professor at Thompson Rivers University and director of the center, for giving us access to the textbook and giving us suggestions for our effort.

Tribal leaders and citizens of Indian nations who live with the remnants of colonial rule have also taught us a great deal about what it takes to renew Indigenous economies. In particular, Joseph Austin, Adam Crepelle, Manny Jules, Michael LeBourdais, David Sickey, Ernest Sickey, Sheldon Spotted Elk, and Bill Yellowtail, to mention a few, have been our teachers. It is unfortunate that their classrooms are reservations where poverty is the norm rather than the exception. May this volume change that.

The Hoover Project on Renewing Indigenous Economies has been financed by "investors" who believe that these ideas can make a difference in Indian Country. First and foremost among these investors are Fritz and Ken Maytag of the Fred Maytag Family Foundation. The Koret Foundation, the Gianforte Family Foundation, the Searle Freedom Trust, the John and Jean De Nault

Family, the Beach Foundation, the Atlas Network, and the Liberty to Grow Foundation have also provided the financial support that has allowed us to produce this book.

Finally, we thank our colleagues who worked with us on this and who take the ideas in this book to another level—Tom Church, Chris Dauer, Shana Farley, Dominic Parker, and Wendy Purnell. They have read drafts, listened to lectures, and produced web-based materials to support the textbook. The Hoover Institution Press editorial team—especially Danica Michels Hodge and Alison Law—has devoted untold hours to make the volume more readable. Finally, special thanks go to Monica Lane Guenther, who proofread every sentence before the press team worked its magic.

PROLOGUE

In light of what we now know about Indigenous economies before contact with European cultures, it is hard to accept that by the late nineteenth century, American law and judicial precedent had institutionalized the status of Native Americans as "wards of the state," incompetents whose well-being was a burden borne of necessity by the United States federal government. The assumption of Indian incompetence might have been understandable had it been the case that Indigenous peoples' standards of living, as reported by the first explorers and settlers, were inferior to those prevalent in England, France, and Spain, but the historical record clearly establishes that they were not. On the contrary, Indian economies were sustainable, and often flourishing, and were able to support civil societies with distinctive arts and industry. Their cultures were no less, and arguably often more, developed than those characteristic of Europe at the time.

As this study will emphasize, it was colonialism—not culture, resources, or innate characteristics—that undermined Native economies and mired Indian people in enervating destitution. Today, American Indians are the poorest of poor minorities, their misery captured in the repetitive collecting of soulless statistics so expected and accepted that they provide little impetus for change. Despite its apparent inability to spark outrage, the data does efficiently capture the heritage of colonialism.

Average household income on Indian reservations was 68 percent below the US average of $53,657 in 2015. Poverty rates are as high as 25 percent and unemployment rates as high as 69 percent. Between 2013 and 2017, median income for Native Americans living on reservations was $29,097 and for all Native Americans (including those living off reservations) was $40,315.[1] This compares to approximately $66,943 for all Americans, $41,361 for African Americans, and $51,450 for Hispanic Americans. The suicide rate among Native Americans has risen 139 percent since 1999, compared to 33 percent for the US population as a whole, according to the Centers for Disease Control and Prevention's National Center for Health Statistics.[2] The rate at which Native American females are raped is 2.5 times the national average.[3] To these statistics add high rates of drug abuse, spousal abuse, and alcoholism.

The stark disparity of Native Americans' dynamic Indigenous past and poverty-burdened present begs for explanation. What caused the demise of traditional Indian economies? Why is contemporary Indian poverty so intransigent? How did it become so entrenched as to lose its urgency and become acceptably normal? What are the barriers to economic growth? And most importantly, once the barriers to progress are named and described, can they then be dismantled and overcome?

There is no simple recipe for renewing Indigenous economies or, for that matter, any economy. Since the publication of Adam Smith's *An Inquiry into the Nature and Causes of the Wealth of Nations* in 1776, economists have struggled to explain the mechanics of prosperity and the dogged persistence of poverty. Early explanations looked for the presence or absence of resources, but counterexamples throughout history and even today—like impoverished, resource-rich Venezuela and thriving, resource-poor Singapore—continuously undermine those theories. Equally, explanations of poverty and prosperity based on the presence or absence of democratic governance founder on the realities of history. Yes, most of the rich countries of the world are democracies, but not all democracies are rich. Consider the list that includes Columbia, South Africa, and the Philippines. And, inconveniently, some nondemocratic countries like China are rapidly becoming richer.[4] Similarly, attempts to tie poverty and prosperity to culture, education, and geographic location fall short of explanatory power.

To be sure, factors like resources, governance, and culture have contributed to the increasing disparity between Indian and White standards of living, even if they have not been determinative of poverty or prosperity. Tribal forms of governance differed greatly from the European centralized models of the White settlers. Many tribes had abundant resources that afforded them sustainable standards of living and even a measure of prosperity, but they could not match the gains in productivity made possible by the Industrial Revolution that was sweeping Europe and imported with the settlers. Eventually, confronted with the well-organized and technologically advantaged standing army of the United States, even the most prosperous of American tribes were relegated to reservations, where their traditional cultures and institutions proved ill-fitted to confinement. Some tribes did try to adapt their institutions to the constraints of reservation life, but they were thwarted by a federal bureaucracy bent on culture-destroying assimilation.

As economists, political scientists, and lawyers gain better understanding of the institutions that govern interactions between individuals, families, firms, and political jurisdictions, religious and culturally focused explanations of poverty on modern reservations are being supplanted. Instead, focus has concentrated on how institutional "rules of the game," like cultural norms and both formal and informal definitions of acceptable behavior, impede or encourage economic growth. Key insights gleaned from this focus include the recognition that incentives shape behavior not just in the economy but also in government; that property rights to land, capital, and labor shape incentives; and that entrepreneurship plays a crucial role in dealing with dynamic resource endowments, technology, and information flows. All of these interactions take place in cultural settings that affect how well or poorly the institutions work to promote economic growth and prosperity.

This book applies the insights of institutional analysis to the stubborn intransigence of poverty in Indian Country, in the belief that obstacles can be overcome only after they have been identified and can be observed in operation. Explaining Indian poverty as the result of "institutional weakness" may bring nods of understanding from academics, but it offers no clarity to the Indian individuals or groups who cannot get loans because the bank will not accept a house on reservation land as collateral, or to the tribe that cannot develop its vast mineral resources because investors hesitate to cross reservation boundaries. Instead, this book looks inside the institutional framework to identify, explain, and give examples of specific rules of the game that frustrate the climb out of poverty, as well as examples of success in changing the rules or addressing the burdens the existing rules impose. Recognizing that investment is prerequisite to economic growth, it focuses on the investment climate in Indian Country, identifying specific circumstances that deter investment both by tribes and tribal members and by off-reservation companies and entrepreneurs.

The intent is to talk plainly about the everyday problems created by differences in the rules of the game on Indian reservations and the rest of the American economy. Talking about "ownership" or "property" or "law and order" among American Indians from a variety of tribes is, for example, tantamount to talking about "football" to American, Australian, and British players as if it were the same game. All name it and claim it, but the rules, the organization, the arenas—indeed, the footballs themselves—are so different that even the most talented of athletes would struggle to move from the gridiron to the soccer field to the rugby arena. And yet, in many ways, the ability to move successfully between games with different rules played in different arenas is what we expect from investors and entrepreneurs, key players in the game of tribal economic growth and development.

The five chapters in this study highlight this unrealistic expectation by identifying and explaining the effect that differing rules of the game have had historically, and continue to have today, on the efforts of Indigenous peoples to use their resources to improve their lives and well-being.

- Chapter 1 establishes that, contrary to popular belief, Indian peoples of the Americas lived in comfort comparable to that of their European contemporaries.
- Chapter 2 explains how colonialism imposed insurmountable costs on Indian economies by changing the rules of the game in ways that severely limited Indians' abilities to adapt.
- Chapter 3 examines the concept of ownership, specifically identifying the differences in Indian and non-Indian Americans' conceptions of rights to use and hold land and other property, and how those differences affect incentives to use resources productively.
- Chapter 4 analyzes how differences in law, enforcement, and collective decision making through government differ on and off reservations and how these differences—lack of business codes and weak courts and enforcement mechanisms, for example—generate conflict and deter investment.
- Chapter 5 describes the practical realities—from the absence of reservation banks to the distance between ATMs—that deter Indian entrepreneurs, and the rules that prevent individuals and tribes from engagement in growth-producing enterprise, deter potential outside investment, and enable exploitation.

Recent policy has encouraged tribes to reclaim authority over their economies, but simply replacing Bureau of Indian Affairs control with tribal council control is not sufficient for economic renewal, as bureaucratic oversight and indifference to Indian input are not the only roadblocks. Tribes often struggle with internal barriers. Tribal governments, for example, are often not inclusive of all tribal members and certainly not of nonmembers. Additionally, many lack the sovereign power to establish a rule of law that is consistent with tribal culture but also comprehensive enough to facilitate trade and commerce in off-reservation national or global economies.

Despite the difficulties, more and more Indian nations are finding paths out of this morass. They are eschewing grants from their federal guardian and, instead, building self-sufficiency by generating revenue. In many cases, the revenues are from gaming, but a significant number of tribes are moving to develop natural resources like coal and oil that underlie their reservations. Examples include the Winnebago, Coushatta, and Southern Ute Tribes, who have diversified their portfolios to generate profits that are then invested in infrastructure, such as schools and health care, and in education that is rejuvenating tribal languages, arts, and culture.

By identifying the institutions that allowed Native Americans to thrive before being colonized and explaining how the institutional rules of colonialism reduced them to dependency on the federal government, this book is intended to encourage a future where individual and tribal entrepreneurship and sovereignty lead to prosperity and, more importantly, to dignity. There is no single path back to the future; the way will be unique to each and every tribe. Understanding the past and the present, however, can help Indians to navigate the path and to cope with its inevitable twists and turns.

1

TRADITIONS OF WEALTH CREATION

The history of Indigenous economies in the Americas presents a puzzle: the societies encountered by the first Europeans were generally prosperous, but Indian peoples today are devastatingly poor.[1] We first address that archaeological and historical reality by demonstrating that precontact American Indian cultures did, indeed, generate wealth. We then explore why they have lost that ability, and whether it can be revived.

The prevailing stereotype among non-Native Americans is that Indian poverty is both endemic and hopeless. As travel and communication increased throughout the twentieth century, the stereotype was strengthened by firsthand experience and shared stories. Although its implications about Indians' cultural competence, adaptability, and resilience wither under scrutiny, the stereotype does accurately reflect that poverty is a persistent reality for most American Indians. The average household income on Indian reservations was 68 percent below the US average of $53,657 in 2015. Twenty percent of Indian households made less than $5,000 annually, compared to 6 percent for the overall US population, and 25 percent were below the poverty level compared to 15 percent for the nation as a whole. Data on poverty-related socioeconomic problems make the comparison even more stark. The suicide rate among Native American males aged fifteen to thirty-four is 1.5 times greater than that of the general population; the rate at which Native American females are raped is 2.5 times the national average; and the rate of child abuse on reservations is twice the national average.[2]

Such socioeconomic conditions were not the norm for Native Americans prior to European contact. Like their contemporaries across the Atlantic Ocean, Indigenous Americans labored to produce a modicum of comfort and security for themselves and their families. And like their European counterparts, their success varied. While some Native Americans lived in shining cities, most did not, just as some Europeans lived in castles, but most did not. However, contrary to lore, myth, and misconception, the explorers and early colonists often encountered Indigenous peoples whose standards of living, cultural complexity, and institutional vibrancy rivaled or even surpassed those of Europeans.

The disparity in standards of living emerged later, as colonizers changed the rules of the game under which American Indians interacted with one another and with non-Indians in the late eighteenth and early nineteenth centuries. By the twentieth century, most Indians had been forced onto reservations and saddled with institutions inimical to their customs and cultures and incompatible with wealth creation. As a result, Indian poverty has taken on an aura of inevitability, of hopelessness.

Precontact Standards of Living

In *1491: New Revelations of the Americas before Columbus*, Charles Mann documents the wealth of Native Americans. The Spanish led by Hernán Cortés, for example, were awed by the sophistication and wealth of the Aztecs they encountered in 1519.

Tenochtitlan [built in the middle of a mountain lake] dazzled its invaders—it was bigger than Paris, Europe's greatest metropolis. The Spaniards gawked like yokels at the wide streets, ornately carved buildings, and markets bright with goods from hundreds of miles away. Boats flitted like butterflies around the three grand causeways that linked Tenochtitlan to the mainland. Long aqueducts conveyed water from the distant mountains across the lake and into the city. Even more astounding than the great temples and immense banners and colorful promenades were the botanical gardens—none existed in Europe. The same novelty attended the force of a thousand men that kept the crowded streets immaculate. Streets that weren't ankle-deep in sewage! The conquistadors had never conceived of such a thing.[3]

On his 1523 voyage, the Italian mariner Giovanni da Verrazzano encountered the robust Dawnland (New England coastal) civilization of the People of the First Light. Europeans described them as "strikingly healthy specimens. Eating an incredibly nutritious diet, working hard but not broken by toil, the people of New England were taller and more robust than . . . [the arriving Europeans]." Modern reconstructions of life in Dawnland at the time of contact suggest that its residents "averaged about 2,500 calories per day, better than those usual in famine-racked Europe."[4]

In 1585–86, the English artist John White traveled in current-day North Carolina, memorializing the inhabitants in a series of romanticized paintings. "To his eye, the people of the Carolinas, cultural cousins to the Wampanoag [of New England], were in superb health, especially compared to poorly nourished, smallpox-scarred Europeans. And they lived in what White viewed as well-ordered settlements, with big flourishing fields of maize."[5] In the early seventeenth century, colonial settlers shivered and starved in their poorly constructed hovels, while the Wampanoag lived in *wetus*, dome-shaped dwellings that were covered by mats woven from grass or by birchbark, making them warmer than the colonists' houses.

The reactions of Indigenous tribes to the arriving Europeans further testify that American Indians' lives were certainly no more "primitive" than, and often arguably superior to, those of the newcomers. Eastern tribes bore little resemblance to the naïve, awestruck helpers of the mainstream Thanksgiving story. Indeed, they often regarded the colonists with disdain. Tribes of the old Northwest and Canada thought the French possessed "little intelligence in comparison to themselves." Europeans, Indians told other Indians, were physically weak, sexually untrustworthy, atrociously ugly, and just plain smelly. The British and French, many of whom had not taken a bath in their lives, were amazed by the Indian interest in personal cleanliness. A Jesuit reported that the "savages" were disgusted by handkerchiefs. "They say we place what is unclean in a fine white piece of linen, and put it away in our pockets as something very precious, while they throw it upon the ground."[6] The Micmacs in New Brunswick and Nova Scotia scoffed at the notion of European superiority. If Christian civilization was so wonderful, why were its inhabitants all trying to settle somewhere else?[7]

Also at odds with historical and archaeological evidence is the assumption that Indigenous people were cowed by European technology.

> Contemporary research suggests . . . that natives soon learned that most of the British were terrible shots, from lack of practice—their guns were little more than noisemakers. . . . Colonists in Jamestown taunted the Powhatan in 1607 with a target they believed impervious to an arrow shot. To the colonists' dismay, an Indian sank an arrow into it a foot deep. . . . When Powhatan later captured John Smith, [Harvard historian] Chaplain notes, Smith broke his pistol rather than reveal to his captors "the awful truth that it could not shoot as far as an arrow could fly."[8]

At the same time, Europeans were impressed by Native American technology. They were awed by maize, which yields more grain per acre than any other cereal. Indian moccasins were so much more comfortable and waterproof than stiff, moldering English boots that when colonists had to walk for long distances, their Indian companions often pitied their discomfort and gave them new footwear. Indian birchbark canoes were faster and more maneuverable than any small European boat. In 1605, three laughing Indians in a canoe literally paddled circles around the lumbering dory rowed by traveler George Weymouth and seven other men.[9]

Traditional Indigenous Economies

Indigenous Americans were neither antagonistic to wealth nor ignorant of how wealth is created. The Native American wealth encountered by European explorers did not materialize like manna from nature's bounty; it was the product of human ingenuity, productivity, and exchange. As a result, American Indians did not just survive, they thrived, and appreciation of their ancient heritage can be a strong foundation for Indigenous peoples' economic renewal today.

Former chief of the Canadian Kamloops Indian Band (now Tk'emlúps te Secwépemc) C. T. Manny Jules has long been an active advocate for empowerment of Native peoples through economic development and self-administration based on the successful dynamics of their precolonial cultures. Jules recounts the experience that awakened him to the sophistication of precontact Indigenous institutions.

In autumn 1997, I travelled . . . to eastern Mexico. It was the first time I had been there. The reason I had gone was to visit Chichen Itza, where every year during the spring and fall equinox the sun casts a shadow which resembles a snake descending to the ground. The shadow joins up perfectly with the carved stone snake's head at the base of the pyramid. The pyramids, monuments and other public infrastructure at Chichen Itza were built around 600 AD, or 1,400 years ago.

As I stared, I had an epiphany. Our people built this without the aid of federal government funding. We had governments that financed themselves. Our governments were able to provide the infrastructure and institutions to build a thriving economy that supported millions of us. . . . Market economies were not foreign to us. We created them ourselves. We traded goods over hundreds of miles. . . . Trade cannot be financed without capital. . . . We had to build transportation methods such as boats. We had to build large public buildings and maintain armies to provide order. These required community investments based on a future return to the community and to individuals. . . . We used money such as dentalium shells and wampum strings. We had individual property rights. . . . According to our written history, my community had individual property rights dating back to the early 1800s to specify where our potato crops were.[10]

Although these institutions were undermined by colonization, they remain a part of Indigenous heritage that begs for renewal. As Jules notes, "We achieved success because we created a balance between our individual creativity and our collective responsibility." Or, to put it in the words of his ancestors, "We will make each other good and great."[11] This is a powerful mantra in the struggle for economic revitalization.

Institutions Matter

Manny Jules is describing what economists call *institutions*. He recognizes that institutions adapt and evolve as environmental conditions change, and that they can be destroyed. Understanding institutions and institutional change is key to understanding both the relative prosperity of precolonial Indian tribes and the persistent poverty of today's reservations.

Nobel Prize–winning economic historian Douglass C. North awakened us to the importance of institutions, which he dubbed "the rules of the game."[12] They are the accepted and expected behaviors of social interaction—sets of formal and informal rules that range from the simplicity of table manners to the complexity of electing presidents.

Incentives are the rewards or punishments created by institutions and are inherent to the strength or weakness of any set of rules of the game. Waitstaff in restaurants are rewarded for courtesy and promptness with tips. Businesspeople are rewarded or punished by reputations that attract or repel customers. Families, neighborhoods, and other groups that interact face-to-face have their own rules of the game. In the larger society, markets—our fundamental economic institution—facilitate interactions with strangers. Markets generate wealth because they allow us to enter into exchanges at low cost with an ever-widening circle of people we do not know.

The institutions of our everyday lives were also part and parcel of precontact Native American life. Their norms and customs were not written down and were therefore less formal than laws today, but they were just as important. Whether the institutions were in the form of norms and customs or of more formal rules, they provided incentives for individuals and groups to be productive. Those institutions are *generally* lacking today.

Ownership: A Requirement for Wealth

One characteristic unique to human beings is the notion of what is mine and what is thine. In asserting ownership, individuals claim exclusive use of things and the right to enforce that claim against others. When a precontact Indian said "mine," it meant the same thing that "mine" means to us today. It asserts that the person saying it has a right to use the resource or capital good and to exclude others from use without his or her permission.

Claiming an exclusive right to use something need not mean "mine," singular. "Ours" broadens the claim to include others—the family, clan, or tribe—who collectively hold the right to use. Saying "mine" or "ours" requires the ability to enforce the right to exclude others from using the resource or good. Among the Plains tribes, for example, a tipi typically belonged to the wife as a family leader. It was up to her to determine who had rights of access. A horse was the property of an individual Indian and could not be used as if it were common property. It took strong, well-disciplined horses to run into a stampeding herd and keep up with the stronger buffalo. Such horses required considerable investment by the owner in training and discipline. An owner of a horse might loan it out, but there was an expectation of payment and of restitution if the horse was injured.

At the tribal level, claiming territory and claiming it as "ours" meant the tribe had to keep other tribes out of the territory unless they were invited in. Pekka Hämäläinen, in his book titled *Lakota America*, documents how the Lakota moved from the upper Great Lakes region onto the Great Plains in pursuit of buffalo. In so doing they developed elaborate institutional structures for engaging in warfare to take territory from others or to defend their own territorial boundaries.[13] Similarly, Jonathan Lear, in his book titled *Radical Hope*, explains how the Crow used the coupstick to mark the boundary between territories.

> Each of the clans within the tribe had its own coupstick—and the head of the war party of that clan would carry the coupstick into battle. A fundamental principle of warrior honor was this: if in battle a warrior stuck his stick in the ground, he must not retreat or leave the stick. A Crow warrior must hold his ground or die losing his coupstick to the enemy. . . . The planting of the coupstick was symbolic of planting a tree that could not be felled. In effect it marked the boundary across which a non-Crow must not pass.[14]

The mythical Indian who did not believe in ownership of land and other resources is largely a romantic stereotype, unrecognizable to the people encountered by colonizing Europeans. In modern times this myth has been promoted by an advertisement in which Chief Seattle is quoted, fictitiously, as saying, "All things are connected like the blood which unites one family. How can you buy or sell the sky, the warmth of the land? The idea is strange to us."[15] Yet the words in the oft-quoted speech are not his. They were written by Ted Perry, a scriptwriter who paraphrased a translation of the speech by William Arrowsmith, a professor of classics. Perry's version added ecological imagery, according to one historian who has researched the subject.[16] The speech reflects a romantic view of Native Americans as stewards of the Earth based on spiritual beliefs—which did undoubtedly play a role—rather than on ownership institutions that rewarded good stewardship.

The myth of nonownership or totally communal ownership by American Indians was also promoted by European governments wanting to use the doctrine of discovery to establish sovereignty over vast tracts of land. Under the legal notion of terra nullius, meaning land is deemed to be unoccupied or uninhabited, the colonies used the doctrine of discovery to justify claiming land. Robert Miller reports a Virginia Company chaplain questioning the morality of occupying Native American lands—"By what right or warrant can we enter into the land of these Savages [and] take away their rightful inheritance?"[17] The answer was terra nullius, meaning there was no need to trade with the Indians because the land was not theirs in the first place.

The mythically expedient assumption that Indians did not understand or utilize ownership ignored the fact that Indigenous peoples identified as personal property that which required a significant amount of time to produce and maintain. Ownership was an incentive to invest time and skill creating capital suited to harvesting the particular resources that sustained the tribe. In the hunting-based economies of the Plains tribes, bows, arrows, arrow-heads, and spears were all privately owned. Marks on arrows identified the hunter or hunters responsible for the kill and entitled him to the animal hide and choice pieces of meat. Throughout Indigenous America, clothes, weapons, utensils, and housing were owned by those who made them—often women.

Native American property rights provided the incentive for capital investments, and the returns on investments provided wealth that could be traded or given away as a matter of reciprocity. For example, rock walls used to channel buffalo over buffalo jumps or weirs to trap spawning fish required significant human investment. This could not occur unless those humans had the capacity to produce surplus food to sustain them while making this investment. Hence, property rights were key to producing surpluses—wealth—that could be consumed or used later.

Roger Williams, founder of Rhode Island, noted that although the Wampanoag lived in a loose scatter, they knew who had the right to use which plots of land, and were "very exact and punctuall [*sic*]" in caring for property lines.[18] Both communal and private property—some formal and some informal—emerged because tribes and individuals benefited from institutions that supported markets, lowered the costs of trade, and helped to prevent the dissipation of scarce, valued resources.

Nomadic tribes practiced systems of use (usufruct) rights to identified territories. It made no sense for roving peoples to "own" land in the way sedentary Europeans did, but it did make sense to define access to hunting, and to award capture rights to successful hunters and trappers. The following are several examples of how tribes did this.

- *Hunting.* The Algonquian Indian tribes who occupied the region of what is now the northeastern United States "carried on their hunting in restricted, family hunting territories descending from generation to generation in the male line."[19] Families protected their territories from trespass and adopted hunting practices that maintained the supply of game. Rights to the location of trap lines were recognized along with the individual ownership of the traps themselves—a property-rights configuration that persisted after European contact into the heyday of the beaver trade.

- *Agriculture.* The Mahican Indians, also in the northeast, practiced hereditary ownership of garden tracts along rivers.
- *Fishing.* Tribes along the Columbia River in the Pacific Northwest established family fishing sites. Fish wheels and weirs were communally constructed. Places along the weir were assigned.[20] Tribes actively managed the native salmon populations, selecting which fish to harvest and which to allow passage upstream to spawn and ensure the health of the fishery in future years. They also had property rights to "clam gardens" created by removing rocks on sandy beaches to make more room for clams. Anthropologist Judith Williams concludes that "private ownership would appear to be a key to the amount of work undertaken making a clam garden."[21]
- *Gathering.* Among California Indian bands, specific piñon, mesquite, and screwbean trees, as well as wild seed patches, were "owned," in that others were excluded from harvesting their produce. Citizens marked their claims with lines of rocks, and clans or tribes punished trespassers.
- *Irrigation.* The Pueblo Indians of the upper Colorado River Basin practiced irrigated agriculture through a mixture of communal and individual property rights: "Technically, the irrigated farmlands belonged to the Pueblo as a whole. Through assignment by the Isleta governor, an individual usually obtained a single acre of land [and the necessary water rights], but if the governor or his captains found that the assignee left the land within a year or did not farm it, the

plot and accompanying water rights were returned to Pueblo possession. . . . The Hopi assigned exclusive rights to fields to . . . matrilineal clans" who marked their lands with boundary stones.[22]

Specialization and Trade

Markets are social institutions in which both formal and informal rules of the game emerge to facilitate and support trade. They exist whenever and wherever buyers and sellers engage in voluntary exchange and are pervasive throughout time and across locations. Historically they have emerged and spread as the promise of mutual benefit created powerful incentives for voluntary exchange among an ever-broadening circle of friends, neighbors, and strangers. The incentive to engage in voluntary exchange is the anticipation of being better off as a result of the trade, a reward expected by both parties in an exchange. If either party expects no benefit, no exchange will take place.

Adam Smith's enduring contribution to our understanding of economics was explaining how and why markets based on voluntary trade make individuals and societies wealthier. In *An Inquiry into the Nature and Causes of the Wealth of Nations*, he argued that markets improve citizens' well-being, no matter their rank or position in society, by expanding their choices about how to earn and what to consume. He identified the source of this market magic as human beings' natural tendency to specialize and trade, or as he put it, "the propensity to truck, barter, and exchange one thing for another is common to all men, and to be found in no other race of animals."[23]

Long before Native Americans encountered Europeans and before any of them might have read Adam Smith, they recognized that specialization is the process of limiting production to specific goods or services in order to increase output by lowering costs and encouraging innovation, and that trade—voluntary exchange—based on specialization gives people access to the things they do not or cannot produce for themselves. By freeing individuals from having to produce everything they consume, trade generates greater wealth, whether material, cultural, or spiritual.

Specialization and exchange are basic human instincts, not unique features of political systems. People do not have to be taught how to create markets, nor must they be able to quote Adam Smith in order to reap benefits from participating in them. If the institutional rules of the game allow it, they discover on their own that specialization and trade serve their self-interest. Such was clearly the case for Indigenous peoples, who created sophisticated trade networks long before Europeans crossed the Atlantic Ocean. By itself, specialization increases production, but it only generates wealth when it results in a surplus that can be traded. If you give up hunting to specialize in bow-making, you must trade in order to eat.

Indigenous people in the Americas specialized and traded both within and between tribes. To maximize the benefits of trade, they specialized in the goods and services they could produce at lower cost than their trading partners. Economists call this ability to produce at lower cost a comparative advantage. As table 1.1 illustrates, some comparative advantages derived from a tribe's natural resource environment (fishing, whaling, iron mining); some from traditions that passed on unique labor skills (hunting, agriculture); and some from location, technology, or innovation (canoes, baskets, pemmican).

With surpluses from specialization, tribes established extensive trade networks, as the following examples illustrate:

- *Trade across the Pacific.* Excavation of the Monks Mound along the Mississippi River has uncovered fossilized sharks' teeth imbedded in wooden clubs. Since no such teeth exist in the region, they are thought to have come from the Hawaiian Islands where sharks' teeth clubs were common. This suggests

14 *Renewing Indigenous Economies*

TABLE 1.1. Examples of Precontact Specialization

Indigenous Group	Specialization
Assiniboine	Animal hide preparation
Blackfoot	Elk-antler hunting bows
Chipewyan	Ice fishing, wheat agriculture
Chumash (Channel Islands)	Plank canoes, shell-bead currency, chert blades, transport services
Copper Eskimos	Copper & soapstone
Haida	Tobacco
Hidatsa & Mandan	Corn*
Iroquois	Clay pipes,[†] maple products, tobacco
Kwakiutl	Woodworking, iron extraction
Menominee (Great Lakes)	Sturgeon, clay pottery, wooden bowls, sisal baskets
Nootka	Whaling, seal & otter hunting
Ojibwa	Beaver trapping
Paleo-Indians	Quartzite for projectile points & tools[‡]
Salish (Coast)	Dugout canoes, salmon, oolichan (fish) oil, dentalium, sea otter fur
Salish (Great Lakes)	Copper, copper spear points & blades, copper beads
Salish (interior—Montana, SW, California)	Obsidian, flint, turquoise, abalone, pearl, squash, beans, rice, quinoa, maple, tobacco
Shoshone (Mountain)	Bighorn sheep horn bows*
Sioux (Lakota)	Buffalo meat & tanned hides
Tlingit	Copper extraction
Tsimshian	Abalone shell harvesting

* Samuel Western, "Trade among Tribes: Commerce on the Plains before Europeans Arrived," WyoHistory.org, April 26, 2016, https://www.wyohistory.org/encyclopedia/trade-among -tribes-commerce-plains-europeans-arrived.

† "Iroquois—Economy," Countries and Their Cultures, last accessed July 15, 2021, https://www .everyculture.com/North-America/Iroquois-Economy.html.

‡ "Spanish Diggings," UltimateWyoming.com, last accessed July 15, 2021, http://ultimatewyoming .com/sectionpages/sec6/extras/spanishdiggings2.html.

that trade across the Pacific Ocean and then across the North American continent predates European contact.[24]

- *Mayan trade network.* The precontact Mayan civilization extended through present-day Guatemala, Belize, El Salvador, Honduras, and parts of Mexico. Inland pathways and water routes in the Gulf of Mexico and the Gulf of Honduras facilitated trade between the Northern Lowlands and the Highlands divisions of the Maya. The Highlands Maya exported corn, fruit, cacao, flint, game, cotton, cloth, obsidian, metates, manos, and various manufactured goods. The Northern Lowlands Maya exported honey, salt, ceramics, various tools, salted fish, marine shells, dye, incense, jade, and rubber.

- *Pipestone network in North America.* Pipes used in religious and civic ceremonies by Indigenous peoples in the upper midwestern United States were commonly made from pipestone, a soft rock metamorphosed from the mud of ancient seabeds. The only known precontact pipestone mine is located in what is now Pipestone National Monument, Minnesota. Pipes were widely traded; archaeological surveys have found pipestone artifacts in South Dakota, Ohio, and Kansas.

- *Nootka–Kwakiutl trading.* The Nootka in the Pacific Northwest specialized in whaling, trading food products like blubber, meat, and oil. Their primary trade partners, the Kwakiutl, were located to the northeast on present-day Vancouver Island. They also traded knives, chisels, nails, buttons, iron, carved spears, fishhooks, and other such implements through a sophisticated network, obtaining resources not present in their homelands by trading with the Coast Salish people.

Another indication of just how prevalent trade was between Native Americans and Europeans comes from the Hudson's Bay Company publication of the exchange rate between beaver pelts

TABLE 1.2. Made-Beaver Pricing at Hudson's Bay Company Post

Commodity	York Factory Prices in Made Beaver, 1740	Fort Albany Prices in Made Beaver, 1733
1 gun	14	10 to 12
1 pistol	7	4
1 blanket	7	1
1 knife	0.250	0.125
1 hat	4	1
1 file	1	1
20 fishhooks	2	1
1 gallon of brandy	4	1
1 pair of looking glasses	1	0.5
1 ice chisel	1	0.5
1 yard of cloth	3.5	0.5
1 shirt	2.5	0.5
1 kettle	2	1

Sources: Hudson's Bay Company, "History of HBC: Fur Trade," accessed 2013, http://www .hbc.com/hbcheritage/history/business/fur/standardtrade.asp; and Ann M. Carlos and Frank D. Lewis, "The Economic History of the Fur Trade: 1670 to 1870," EH.net Encyclopedia, ed. Robert Whaples. March 16, 2008, https://eh.net/encyclopedia/the-economic-history-of -the-fur-trade-1670-to-1870.

and other trade goods. The *made beaver* (a male beaver pelt used as a unit of account by the Hudson's Bay Company) became the medium of exchange and standard of value in Indigenous trade with first the French and later the English. The made beaver as a unit of currency was used to value other animal pelts—otter, squirrel, and moose—and to value European goods Indians purchased, as shown in table 1.2. The value of made beaver varied with both market conditions in Europe and with the degree of competition among colonial traders. For example, significant increases in the price of furs between 1732 and 1756 at York Factory and Fort Albany in Canada were the result of higher prices in London and Paris and greater French presence within the main fur-trading areas.

Trade Infrastructure

Transportation and communications infrastructure lowers the costs of trade, but is unlikely to be constructed by individual traders. Because they cannot capture all the benefits of their investment, entrepreneurs rarely fund highway construction, for example. Because the benefits can be captured by people other than those making the investment, roads and similar infrastructure are provided collectively through the public sector. Indigenous peoples recognized that the disparity between private and public benefits was best addressed collectively. Through their governments they funded, built, and maintained trail networks, water routes, and, in the case of the Maya, even storehouses and rest stops.

Oolichan—also known as eulachon or candlefish—was harvested by Indigenous peoples along the Pacific Coast from Northern California to Alaska. The oolichan grease or oil was used as salve, sauce, seasoning, food preservative, laxative, lamp oil, and leather-tanner. It was a source of vitamins A, C, and E, and was used as medicine to treat colds and flu. According to Fisheries and Oceans Canada, "one box of grease could be bartered for four blankets, two beaver skins, or two boxes of dried halibut. . . . [Two boxes] of grease had the value of one canoe." The grease was so highly valued that a comprehensive network of publicly maintained footpaths known as grease trails facilitated trade between coastal and inland peoples across Vancouver Island, from the Yukon to Northern California, and east into central Montana and Alberta. Between 1821 and 1846, the grease trails were converted into fur trails as the demand for fur outpaced the demand for oil.[25]

Like roads, trading centers lowered transaction costs by providing a node for gathering. In their book *Commerce by a Frozen Sea*, economists Ann Carlos and Frank Lewis describe the extensive trade networks that developed in Canada along Hudson Bay.[26] There, Indians specialized in trapping and traded for needles, guns, axes, and textiles with the Hudson's Bay Company, which had an extensive network of trading posts. Similarly, on the upper Missouri, the Mandan, Hidatsa, and Arikara villages became trading nodes. Foods such as corn, beans, and squash from farming villages were exchanged for dried meats and hides. Historian James Ronda points out that these villages were the "great Missouri River country store that attracted so many Europeans, as well as Indians. The transactions at this crossroads of cultures and goods touched the lives of people far from central North Dakota and in turn conditioned the Mandans' and the Hidatsas' relations with all outsiders."[27]

After contact, the existing Indigenous infrastructure adapted to trade in European goods, horses, and guns. To appreciate the extent of the North American trading networks, consider how far and how fast items crossed the continent. The Lewis and Clark expedition traded war hatchets with the Mandan in 1804, and were surprised that one hatchet reached Idaho's Indigenous people before the explorers themselves did. The expedition also encountered Spanish horse gear in the upper Missouri and British teapots on the Columbia—a testament to the reach of the upper Missouri trade network.

In Peru, the ancient Norte Chico civilization was supported by trade in cotton and seafood through what may have been the first modern form of government in the Western Hemisphere. The Inca constructed one of the most extensive pre-Columbian road and trail systems in South America, despite the fact that they did not have horses or wheeled vehicles. While most of the roads were essentially dirt paths, there were stone-paved sections and, in some areas, suspension bridges over ravines and bodies of water. The trails were intended to be traveled on foot by llamas packed with trade goods. In Central America, the Maya built public warehouses, trade routes including stone roads, and rest houses for traders.

Traditional Capital Markets

Markets do not operate in a vacuum. Initiating and sustaining economic growth requires institutions that support specialization and voluntary trade and that increase production. Almost everything that is produced requires physical and human capital, so economic growth depends on continual capital improvement and accumulation—from land, buildings, tools, and technology to the skills of people who design, build, and operate machinery and software, and who organize and innovate. It is difficult to accumulate capital without property rights, stable government, and sound banking and financial systems.

D. Bruce Johnsen is one of the few scholars to study the financial systems embedded in potlatch ceremonies of Native Americans.[28] In the Pacific Northwest, the potlatch was an opulent ceremonial feast at which possessions were given away. The motive for the potlatch presumed by Western scholars before Johnsen was to enhance the prestige of the wealthy giver. Johnsen hypothesizes that the potlatch was instead motivated by "institutionalized reciprocity," which provided capital from the giver to those who received it in return for future exchanges when the givers might find themselves less well-off. The gifts also secured from the receiver an agreement not to take resources, especially spawning salmon, from the giver's territory.

Johnsen quotes from anthropologist Franz Boas to show just how sophisticated the potlatch capital market was. As with a modern-day loan for a car or a house, the lender practiced due diligence by assessing the borrower's credit rating, and the potlatch "gift" came with an interest payment attached to it. As Boas wrote:

> For a period of a few months, for 5 borrowed blankets 6 must be returned . . . for a period of six months, for 5 borrowed blankets 7 must be returned . . . for a period of twelve months or longer, for 5 borrowed blankets 10 must be returned. . . .

When a person has a poor credit, he may pawn his name for a year. Then the name must not be used during that period, and for 30 blankets which he has borrowed he must pay 100 in order to redeem his name. . . .

The rate of interest . . . varies somewhat around 25 per cent, according to the kindness of the loaner and the credit of the borrower. For a very short time blankets may be loaned without interest.[29]

Throughout North and South America, various forms of money helped facilitate capital markets. In the Pacific Northwest, copper plates, known as "coppers," were used. Boas concludes that "coppers have the same function which bank notes of high denominations have with us. The actual value of the piece of copper is small, but it is made to represent a large number of blankets and can always be sold for blankets."[30] Wampum and wampum belts consisting of hand-hewn white shell beads from the North Atlantic channeled whelk and purple beads from the western North Atlantic hard-shelled clam were used as money by northeastern Indians before European contact. After contact, the first colonists adopted wampum as a currency for trading with Native Americans. In South America, the quipu consisted of a long rope with multiple and variously colored pendant strings tied to it.[31] According to Johnsen, the quipu was a means of numeric accounting. Johnsen's hypothesis is that the quipu served in part as a form of double-entry bookkeeping and possibly also as records of indebtedness similar to modern warehouse receipts, with grain held in storage as the underlying good. Lacking the wheel and functional beasts of burden, transportation in the extensive and rugged Incan, Aztec, and Mayan Empires was slow, laborious, and costly. Nobility who wanted to conduct transactions in distant places would have vastly preferred to transfer warehouse receipts than grain itself.

The conclusion from this evidence is that Native North and South Americans fully understood the need for capital investment and for currency and accounting that would reduce the cost of market transactions. Without capital markets—i.e., wealth produced, saved, and invested in future productivity—how could these "primitive" societies have built the Maya, Aztec, and Inca pyramids; the Anasazi cliff dwellings; or the Monks Mound? In short, Native Americans were capitalists.

Jurisdiction and Governance

Whether it is a matter of enforcing individual ownership claims, protecting borders of territories, or organizing tribes for the production of public goods (such as roads, meeting halls, or irrigation systems for which it is difficult to exact payment from users), collective action requires an institutional structure that allows the government to act. Clarifying who has jurisdiction over what is prerequisite for trade and institutional infrastructure. Stable governance based on the rule of law reduces uncertainty about the future and therefore the risk of investing in capital and participating in markets.

Traditional Indigenous governments exercised their fiscal power to tax by compelling individuals to give up some of their wealth for the benefit of the larger society. Taxation was the source of funding for most public infrastructure even before European colonization. Tax systems ranged from the potlatch wealth redistribution practiced in the Pacific Northwest to tribute payments that financed Mayan infrastructure.

The complex jurisdictional framework of the Aztec Empire included an efficiently administered tax system that funded the sophisticated infrastructure of trade. Aztec city-states were independently organized societies ruled by kings who controlled the land. Kings designated temple sites and granted estates to high lords who divided the land among their wards, who then assigned plots to commoner families. Lords reassigned land if it was abandoned or neglected, or if a user died without heirs. Farmers could sell use-rights to their plots, but the land still belonged to the king and remained under the jurisdiction of the ward and city-state. Commoners paid a form of tax or tribute to the high lords who, in turn, paid tribute to the king, usually in the form of goods, including textiles and clothing, food, military supplies, building materials, and animal products. At other times commoners paid their taxes with their labor on large public projects and temples.

Public infrastructure funded by taxation helps to increase market size, which in turn increases specialization and innovation by reducing production and transportation costs. Producers and traders also depend on governments to provide secure legal environments. Knowing that contracts will be enforced and disputes resolved in independent, reliable courts is critical to their willingness to take on the risks of market endeavors.

The greatest gains from trade emerge in markets with clear rules, effective dispute resolution, and robust enforcement mechanisms, because they help to create certainty. Secure, predictable governance institutions reduce the costs of negotiating transactions, establishing standards, and enforcing agreements. Even something as mundane as establishing standard weights and measures eliminates the transaction costs of producers finding a way to communicate the size of their products, as well as of consumers struggling to figure how much they are buying or to compare similar products.

We can look to Mesoamerica for evidence that Indigenous people understood that markets flourish in an atmosphere where jurisdiction is defined and the rule of law reduces uncertainty. The precontact Aztecs developed a system of commercial law enforced by the *pochteca*, merchants who paid the Aztec government for the power to regulate the marketplace, judge all lawsuits relating to the merchant class, and impose punishments.

Other merchants paid a market tax to *pochteca* judges for permission to participate in and receive assignments to designated areas within the market. Inspectors mixed in the crowds to protect consumers by ensuring that merchants adhered to established exchange rates and that their goods met measurement and quality standards. If inspectors discovered violations, they destroyed the offending merchant's wares and confiscated counterfeit items.

The *pochteca* also presided over commercial courts and adjudicated contracts. The Aztec legal framework differentiated among sales, commissions, leases, work, and loan contracts. All contracts were created orally and became binding when witnessed by four people. Collateral was in the form of goods, property, or a promise to become a slave upon default.

Those accused of violations by market inspectors appeared before panels of judges for determination of guilt and for sentencing. Commercial courts governed all contract disputes as well as disagreements that arose in the marketplace or involved *pochteca* citizens. Those convicted of crimes were fined and their families were held responsible for payment. Restitution was common in minor theft, fraud, or personal-injury cases. In serious cases, the offender was made the slave of the victim, or was beaten to death in the center of the marketplace as a warning to others.

Of equal sophistication in North America was the layered jurisdictional framework of the League of Five Nations, also known as the Haudenosaunee or, as the colonists called it, the Iroquois League. The League was a loose alliance among the Oneida, Mohawk, Seneca, Cayuga, and Onondaga tribes governed by the Great Law of Peace.

> Striking to the contemporary eye, the 117 codicils of the Great Law [of Peace] were concerned as much with establishing limits on the great council's powers as on granting them. Its jurisdiction was strictly limited to relations among the nations and outside groups; internal affairs were the province of the individual nations. . . . According to the Great Law, when the council of sachems was deciding upon "an especially important matter or a great emergency," its members had

to "submit the matter to the decision of their people" in a kind of referendum.

In creating such checks on authority, the league was just the most formal expression of a region-wide tradition. The sachems of Indian groups on the eastern seaboard were absolute monarchs in theory. In practice, wrote colonial leader Roger Williams, "they will not conclude of ought . . . unto which the people are averse." The league was predicated, in short, on the consent of the governed, without which the entire enterprise would collapse. Compared to the despotic societies that were the norm in Europe and Asia, Haudenosaunee was a libertarian dream.[32]

In *Lakota America*, Hämäläinen describes how the Lakota evolved from a hunter-gatherer tribe of the upper Great Lakes to one of the most powerful nations west of the Mississippi. As they moved from the Great Lakes region carrying firearms, the Lakota took control of trade in the Missouri Valley and, ultimately, with the horse, control of the high plains. Along the Missouri, they charged tolls to those moving furs and trade goods; where buffalo were plentiful, they excluded other tribes from hunting; and to add cultivated crops such as corn to their diets, they established trade agreements with less nomadic tribes.

All of this required complicated governance structures at different levels ranging from the nation to the band. The nation was not "a formal state or confederacy" but was instead "a manifestation of deep voluntary attachments that bound the seven fires [tribes] together . . . from the bottom up, with language and kinship as the main cohesive."[33] At the lower end were smaller groups in which "individuals, families, and bands moved around constantly, arranging themselves into different constellations as circumstances demanded . . . creating a thick lattice of kinship ties that transcended local and regional identities."[34] The bottom-up structure limited the power of the chiefs and councils, but they did have the power to organize large armies, with the consent of the subgroups, for the purpose of defending or expanding their territories.

Hämäläinen succinctly explains why and how the ways the Lakota enforced rules on the inside had the added benefit of helping to protect them from invaders on the outside. The rules within the tribe provided incentives for individuals, families, and clans to make investments in their personal wealth that allowed them to thrive in new territories and to trade with other tribes when gains from trade were available. Furthermore, those investments, especially in equestrian skills, provided the human and physical (horse) capital that could be called on by war leaders to protect tribal territories and acquire new lands. Hämäläinen summarizes by saying the Lakota went to war "to protect their lands, to exact revenge, to secure hunting and trading privileges, to enhance their power and prestige by taking slaves, [and] to preempt threat."[35]

Fiscal Authority and Money

In modern economies, banks, insurance companies, and other financial institutions facilitate the creation of capital and sharing of risk. In Indigenous economies, barter in small, face-to-face exchanges served this function. Grain-storage bins, baskets, and structures were ways of storing wealth that could later be traded; they were roughly parallel to current-day savings accounts in banks or financial investments. When we have surplus income, we save it for a rainy day or for a time in the future when we might want to purchase a new house or car. Native Americans also saved for the same reasons.

Although often informal, the financial institutions of many precontact Indigenous trade networks developed forms of money with well-known exchange ratios to reduce transaction costs. Barter was common in Indigenous trade, but as centers and networks grew, so did the burden of the "double coincidence of wants" that limits exchanges to the right two people, with the right products, in the right amounts, in the right place, at the right time. Using a medium of exchange—money—reduced the transaction cost of barter, so Indigenous traders quickly adopted the practice of using a commodity or other item as accepted payment in a given market. Not all Indigenous economies developed money, but those that did benefited from increased trade. Money facilitated indirect and multiparty transactions, which, in turn, encouraged greater specialization, making more goods and services more widely available to more consumers.

On both coasts of North America, shells performed the functions of money, acting as a medium of exchange, a standard of value, and a store of value. Pacific Northwest coastal tribes from what is today Northern California up to southeast Alaska used strings of dentalium shells as a medium of exchange before the coming of European fur traders. The larger an individual shell or the longer a string of shells, the greater the purchasing power. A fathom-long string could buy up to two ocean-traveling canoes, and a fathom-long string plus eight or ten shells was worth a slave or a large sea otter skin. After contact, blankets became the preferred medium of exchange, although dentalium was sometimes still used for smaller transactions between members of different tribes.

"Native American money could involve something that has value in all cultures, such as the Aztec's gold dust, or something that is valued by a particular civilization, such as Mayan coffee beans," according to an online reference.[36] On the other hand, many tribes used items without inherent commodity value, like wampum strings of clam shells. These were initially used by northeastern coastal tribes, but the use of wampum spread after adoption by the prosperous and powerful Iroquois tribes. "Wampum was later used by many colonists as a form of currency. For instance, Peter Stuyvesant paid his workers in wampum when they constructed the New York citadel. The island of Manhattan was purchased for wampum."[37]

Even before colonial settlement, the practice of using a medium of exchange spread widely with the fur trade. To reduce transaction costs and broaden their networks, traders adopted the practice of using Indian-produced commodities like beaver pelts and buckskins as money. The latter gave us the term *buck* as the equivalent of a dollar, when Conrad Weiser, a Pennsylvania Dutch pioneer, wrote in his journal in 1748 that someone had stolen "300 bucks worth of items." He then noted that five bucks were worth a cask of whiskey.[38]

Conclusion

History, anthropology, and archaeology establish the wealth-creating capacity of Indigenous American institutions. Yet, not long after contact, Indian communities entered a period of economic decline that, with few exceptions, continues today. Modern Indigenous populations throughout the Americas are generally the most impoverished groups in their respective countries, but it is worth noting that the institutions that structure their lives today are not those of their heritage.

The purpose of this study is to help tribal leaders and other interested students rediscover that their cultures and traditions need not close the door to economic growth and prosperity. This and the following chapters seek to emphasize that America's Indigenous people created wealth through specialization and trade, recognized the value of property, and developed institutions that helped them create levels of comfort and security found in few other parts of the world, and even some examples of enviable splendor. Wealth-generating institutions were strongest in Central and South America among the Maya, Aztec, Inca, and Norte Chico communities—so strong that they may indeed have been the wealthiest not just in the Western Hemisphere, but in the world. While Indigenous communities in what are now Canada and the United States did not achieve the impressive levels found in Mesoamerica, they did successfully create markets based on specialization and trade that afforded them a standard of living on par with that of their contemporaries in Europe.

Today, the descendants of these once self-sustaining economies are impoverished and dependent, raising the question of what happened between then and now to so starkly reverse their fortunes. The short answer is that the era of colonization destroyed traditional institutions, replacing them with new rules of the game inimical to economic growth and prosperity. We will examine the history of institutional change in the next chapter.

Chapters 3, 4, and 5 will examine, in turn, the institutions of property, jurisdiction and governance, and fiscal and financial power that support markets and economic growth. Each chapter will explain how the rules of the game promote or hinder economic growth, give an overview of institutional conditions in Indian Country today, and identify institutional improvements with significant potential to renew Indian economies. Each chapter will also offer data and contemporary stories of success and failure to illustrate how revitalizing the institutional framework can restart the engine of economic growth, generate business and employment, raise standards of living in Indian communities, and restore dignity for individuals and tribes.

2

TRIBAL ECONOMIES UNDER COLONIALISM

The Southern Ute Reservation sits on massive energy resources, but for most of the last century the small tribe—now numbering fewer than 1,500 members—was impoverished. The prosperous hunters and traders who once roamed the Great Basin were forced onto a reservation spanning about one-third of what would become Colorado, and their strength and wealth quickly dissipated. By 1895, the tribe had been squeezed into a fifteen-by-seventy-five-mile strip, consisting of a mosaic of land tenure including both private property and trust property, the latter being under the control of the federal government. Today those trust parcels make up half of the reservation.[1]

In 1896, the Southern Ute Indian Tribe began the fight to reclaim its sovereignty and economic independence. It was slow going. Throughout the first half of the twentieth century, the reservation remained an island of poverty with high unemployment, little income, and an abysmal standard of living. At midcentury, "homes were small and crowded, in poor condition, and almost universally lacking in sanitation systems, clean drinking water, electricity, and telephones."[2]

It took over a century, but the Southern Utes persevered, slowly winning court judgments to reclaim their water, land, and mineral rights and gradually loosening the hold of the federal bureaucracy over their economic future. As a result of tribal control of resources, revenue from five tribal energy companies is invested in the Southern Ute Growth Fund, estimated to be worth $4 billion, and dividends from the fund are distributed annually to tribal members. Because of the tribe's natural resource endowments, "each of its 1,400 members is a millionaire many times over, on paper anyway."[3]

The history of the Southern Utes' struggle for sovereignty and economic renewal is instructive; its length and complexity illustrate why so few other tribes have similar success stories to tell. With significant stores of coal, oil, and gas beneath the reservation, the tribe seemed poised to benefit from the post–World War II energy boom, but the benefits consistently fled the reservation. High-bidder leases were awarded to off-reservation energy companies by the Department of the Interior, with essentially no tribal input. In the 1950s and early 1960s, revenue was routinely and systematically stolen from the tribe, fraud was rampant, and developers were unintimidated by lackadaisical government oversight.

Change began with Leonard Burch and Sam Maynes, new leaders who were determined to capture the benefits of the energy market. Burch was elected tribal chairman in 1966, and in 1968 he brought on Maynes, his lifelong friend, as general counsel. Prior to their tenure, the tribe was receiving less than $500,000 per year in oil and gas royalties, a fraction of the oil company's profits. Maynes advised the tribal council to place a moratorium on all new oil and gas leasing. To have more clout, the tribe joined twenty-four others to form the Council of Energy Resource Tribes. This started the Southern Utes' long climb out of poverty and paternalism.

Writing for the *High Country News*, Jonathan Thompson, who lived on the reservation for forty years, describes how the "Southern Utes became part of a widespread transformation of federal energy policy," culminating in 1982 with congressional passage of the Indian Mineral Development Act, which gave tribes the authority to negotiate their own mineral leases. As a result, "The tribe negotiated more favorable leases with outside companies and enacted a severance tax on gas production. . . . The tribe's energy department also took over the auditing of leasing from the feds, a move made by only a handful of other tribes, which helped uncover potential cheating."[4]

With more control of its own destiny, the tribe took the courageous but risky step in 1992 of starting its own gas production company, using an $8 million court settlement against the federal government. The investment paid off. Red Willow Production Company has since grown into an oil and gas exploration and production conglomerate, and the tribe has diversified its economy by investing in other enterprises, ranging from a gambling casino and hotel to biofuel production.

With profits from oil and gas production, the tribe was able to take control of and manage the reservation's infrastructure. It runs the medical clinic, formerly operated by the Indian Health Service. It built a state-of-the-art recreation center and introduced a Ute-language program in its schools. The tribe's Southern Ute Community Action Program provides alcohol- and substance-abuse treatment centers, a senior citizen center, and job-training programs. Oil and gas profits provide scholarships for every tribal member who wants to attend college. The Southern Utes distribute dividends to every tribal member between the ages of twenty-six and fifty-nine and retirement benefits to those over sixty. Thompson reports that "the numbers vary year by year and the tribe won't reveal them, but one Southern Ute in his 70s says his share last year [2009] totaled $77,500."[5]

Southern Utes' struggle for economic independence and sovereignty was the legacy of nineteenth-century Indian policy that made tribes "domestic dependent nations." This chapter explains why the renewal of the Southern Ute economy has taken so much time, courage, and persistence, and why it is so difficult for other tribes to replicate their startling economic growth. As attorney Joseph Austin, citizen of the Navajo Nation, puts it, "It's like climbing Mt. Everest and we've been hiking for decades."[6] That mountain is so high because of imperialistic nineteenth-century laws and Supreme Court decisions and bureaucratic "white tape," as Earnest Sickey, former chairman of the Coushatta Tribe of Louisiana, calls it. Climbing the mountain requires building mutually reinforcing internal economic and governance institutions that foster specialization and wealth-creating trade under the umbrella of tribal sovereignty. It is time to start the climb.

Colonizing Indian Country

When the first Europeans stepped off their boats, they were greeted by Native Americans (not Indians from India) who by and large were friendly and welcoming. For the immigrants, simply standing on terra firma must have been welcome enough, but they got more. They learned much about what the land had to offer and how the Indians could teach them to utilize Nature's bounty. For the Indians, metal tools, pots, and pans were probably the most valuable thing brought by the English. In combination, both parties had ample gains from trade to keep things peaceful.

Trading or negotiating between Indians and Whites was based on individual ownership. "This is my knife and I will trade it for your basket" implies that the trading parties owned the goods (which we saw in chapter 1 was normally the case among precontact Native Americans) and could exchange the right to use the goods.

When it came to land and other resources, however, it was harder to say "this is mine," because land and resources were "ours" where the unit was more often the family, clan, or tribe. As such, individual-to-individual trades of land were difficult because sorting out the Native American side of the trade required negotiating with the collective group. Expanding a territorial border, for example, required agreement from a collective group of American Indians and from colonists who were on a frontier delineated by governments that were not well formed and organized. Hence, the trading was between groups of individuals when land and natural resources were on the table.

The institutional framework within which tribes and potential investors currently operate emerged from more than a century of statute and judicial precedent based on powers granted by the Constitution to the federal government for the purpose of making treaties and regulating commerce with foreign nations— in this case Indian nations. Over time, those powers have been wielded through a dizzying series of inconsistent legislative and administrative decisions. Let us consider the evolution of federal Indian law.

The Marshall Trilogy

The evolution of Indian policy—unlike the Constitution, which emphasized individual rights vis-à-vis the national government— focused on tribes. Indian policy is all about government-to-government relations, and too often ignores individual Indian rights.

Three US Supreme Court decisions in the 1830s, adjudicated under the leadership of Chief Justice John Marshall, stand as the foundation for federal Indian law. These are known as the Marshall Trilogy.

- *Johnson v. M'Intosh* (1823). The Supreme Court ruled that private citizens could not purchase lands from Native Americans, therefore asserting that Native Americans did not own their tribal land. Further restricting Native American tribes' ability to sell land to private parties enabled the US government to acquire tribal land at the lowest possible cost.

- *Cherokee Nation v. Georgia* (1831). The Cherokee Nation sued the state of Georgia for passing laws that would have "annihilated" the tribe, which it argued was a "foreign nation in the sense of our constitution and law." Georgia countered that the Cherokee could not sue because the Cherokee could not be a foreign nation, because the tribe had no written constitution or strong central government. The Cherokee wanted the US Supreme Court to void all Georgia law that extended to the tribe and its lands. The court, however, refused to evaluate the case because the tribe was a "domestic, dependent nation." This ruling set the precedent that relations between tribes were to be with the federal, not state, government and established that tribes and their citizens were dependent on the United States government as would be a "ward to its guardian."

- *Worcester v. Georgia* (1832). This decision laid out the legal relationship among the federal government, the states, and the tribes. The ruling effectively stated that the federal government, not local or state governments, held the sole authority for dealing with Native American nations. The domestic dependency terminology that emerged from the Marshall court in the early nineteenth century limits tribal sovereignty to that of a ward under protection of the guardian federal government.

Following the Indian Wars of the late nineteenth century, when Native Americans were relegated to reservations, the Marshall Trilogy provided the bases for imposing rules from Washington, DC, and for holding Indian lands in trust by the federal guardian on behalf of its Indian wards. These rules and trusteeship supplanted traditional laws and customs. In short, federal Indian law replaced tribal law.

Federal Indian Law

The Constitution and the Marshall Trilogy are the foundation of federal Indian law, in contrast to tribal law, which consists of the laws and customs internal to the tribes. Four themes have consistently formed the doctrinal basis of federal Indian law throughout American history, even as it evolved to serve a variety of governmental and political purposes:

1. Indian tribes, the fundamental units of Indian law, "are sovereign entities with inherent powers of self-government."
2. Congress, through its power to regulate and modify the status of tribes, limits tribal sovereignty.
3. Only the federal government has the power to deal with tribes unless Congress explicitly delegates powers to state governments.
4. The federal government is responsible for protecting tribes and tribal property from state and local governments and from citizens.[7]

The Constitution gives Congress the power to regulate commerce with Indian tribes, a power it established in the Indian Intercourse Acts (1790, 1793, 1796, 1799, 1802, and 1834) that were designed to deal with ongoing conflicts arising from settlers' encroachment on Indian lands. Congress prohibited the purchase of Indian land without federal government approval, declared the inalienability of Indian title except by treaty, and reinforced the federal government's power to regulate commerce with tribes. All of this was in addition to the Marshall Trilogy, which affirmed Indians' legal, inalienable right to their lands established through occupancy under the British, with the caveat that this right existed only at the sufferance of the newly established US government.[8]

Enforcement of federal Indian law mostly fell on the Bureau of Indian Affairs (BIA), created in 1824 as an agency of the War

Department and transferred in 1849 to the Department of the Interior. The BIA deployed its agents to reservations as local enforcers who oversaw the General Allotment Act (also known as the Dawes Act), passed in 1887, which did more than any other act to hold Native Americans in colonial bondage. With allotment, the federal government reversed its policy of keeping Indian Country separate from the dominant White culture to one of promoting assimilation into that dominant culture by breaking up reservations and allotting small land parcels to individuals. Title to land was to be held in trust for twenty-five years for the purpose of protecting the allottee from state taxation and unscrupulous land dealers during the time the allottee learned how to work the land. After a reservation was "fully allotted," so-called "excess" or "surplus" lands were opened to settlers. Despite what were arguably good intentions, the net effect of the Dawes Act was to reduce the total acreage of Indian land from 138 million to 48 million acres in the period from 1887 to 1934.[9]

Following the General Allotment Act, the Burke Act or Forced Fee Patenting Act of 1906 further ensconced tribes in colonialism by breaking up communal lands and distributing them to individual heads of households. Amazingly, it required that the land be held in trust by the federal government—the guardian for its ward—until the government deemed the landholder to be "competent and capable" before fee simple title would be granted. It also withheld US citizenship for Indians during the "probationary" period of trusteeship.

The Indian Reorganization Act (IRA) or the Wheeler Howard Act of 1934 took a step toward tribal sovereignty by renouncing the assimilationist policy of the previous half century. It ended allotment, supported the continued existence of reservations, restored to tribes some of their lost "surplus" lands, and authorized and actively encouraged tribal self-governance. Tribal constitutions were, however, subject to approval by the Secretary of the Interior and drawn up under the tutelage of the BIA. Unfortunately, the constitutions adopted by most tribes did not reestablish traditional governance structures and, hence, did not provide "the glue" for strengthening tribal sovereignty or laying a foundation for economic development.[10]

From 1953 to 1968, the focus of Indian policy shifted again, reverting to the assimilation of individual Indians and tribes into non-Indian society. Congress authorized termination of tribes' special relationship with the federal government, and the BIA offered grants to individuals to relocate to major urban areas to find employment. Once a tribe was terminated, its members were "subject to the same laws and entitled to the same privileges and responsibilities as are applicable to other citizens of the United States [and were no longer] wards of the United States"[11] In practical terms, this meant that the land of a terminated tribe was privatized and sold. Termination was disastrous for tribes, especially in terms of destruction of the customs, culture, and language that were important parts of the social glue for Native Americans.

The two largest terminations, those of the Klamath of Oregon and the Menominee of Wisconsin, were typical. The Klamath lands were sold and the proceeds quickly dissipated. The Menominee were plunged into even deeper economic trouble than they had previously endured. Not until 1973 were they successful in securing legislation restoring their special relationship with the federal government and placing their lands back in federal trust. The Klamath were less fortunate; their trust relationship eventually was restored but not their lands.[12]

Public Law 280, passed in 1953 and amended in 1958, further reduced the potential for tribal sovereignty by giving the states of California, Nebraska, Minnesota, Oregon, Wisconsin, and Alaska (all with some exceptions) civil and criminal jurisdiction over reservations in the states' boundaries. The 1958 amendment offered all other states the option of assuming similar jurisdiction by statute or state amendment and without consent of the tribes. The states were allowed to choose whether to assume jurisdiction in whole or in part.

While P.L. 280 replaced applicable federal law with state law, it did not end the federal trust relationship, meaning that states could not tax Indian properties or regulate hunting and fishing. Because the states were given new enforcement responsibilities, but not the power to tax tribal properties to cover the increased cost, only ten states (Nevada, Florida, Idaho, Iowa, Washington, South Dakota, Montana, North Dakota, Arizona, and Utah) pursued this jurisdictional change.[13]

The effects of P.L. 280 are debated. To be sure, it was a restriction on tribal sovereignty imposed by politicians in Washington, DC. On the other hand, it provided judicial continuity for tribes lacking judicial systems that could foster the rule of law as applied to business transactions. Anderson and Parker examined the effect on the incomes of seventy-one reservations between 1969 and 1999.[14] They found that income growth was 35 percentage points higher on reservations under state jurisdiction. Their explanation for this higher growth rate is that state jurisdiction provides a more stable climate for business transactions, especially for those businesses contracting with tribes and tribal members.

Consider the example of the Skywalk, built on the Hualapai Indian Reservation. To capitalize on its unique location on the rim of the Grand Canyon, the tribe contracted with Las Vegas developer David Jin to build a tourist attraction called the Skywalk. The $30 million investment in a horseshoe-shaped, crystal-clear glass walkway jutting 70 feet out from the rim of the Grand Canyon opened in 2007 and was an immediate success, with estimated revenues of $5 million per year.

Subsequently, the tribal council alleged that Jin failed to finish the visitor center and exercised its sovereign right of eminent domain to seize the property. Jin contended that the tribe had waived its right to sovereign immunity in the development contract, thus negating its authority to exercise eminent domain. On February 11, 2013, US District Judge David Campbell agreed with Jin, saying that the tribe had "clearly waived its sovereign immunity" and that its legal arguments were "odd," "nonsensical," and "wholly unconvincing."

Rather than accept the decision or pursue the normal appeals processes, the tribal council tried an end run to avoid the $28.6 million judgment by seeking Chapter 11 bankruptcy protection "to prevent further collection efforts" by Jin. They claimed that the tribe owned Grand Canyon Development Corporation and, therefore, that the corporation was protected by sovereign immunity. ·

Eventually the case was settled out of court, but in the meantime the tribe's reputation for future business dealing was tarnished. Louise Benson, who was chair of the tribe when the Skywalk contract was signed, said tribal leaders were "giving the Hualapai a terrible reputation that will injure the tribe for years." She added, "All over Indian Country, I think this is bad."[15] In short, if tribal courts do not establish a reputation for enforcing contracts, their economies will fall behind those that do or those that rely on state jurisdiction under P.L. 280.

This example is neither new nor unique in Indian Country. In 1953, the Jicarilla Apache tribe began negotiating with petroleum companies to explore and produce oil and gas on its reservation. The contracts provided for royalty payments of 12.5 percent. Then, in 1976, after the companies had made significant investments in infrastructure, the tribe added a severance tax, taking the total rate to nearly 20 percent. In court, the companies argued that only state and local authorities had the ability to tax mineral rights on Indian reservations; they eventually lost the argument when the US Supreme Court ruled in favor of the tribe. This judgment, however, did nothing to improve the investment climate for energy development on reservations. With an estimated $1 trillion in recoverable energy reserves under reservation land, tribes with those resources could be rich, but court decisions such as this discourage investors from doing business on reservations.

In an attempt to disentangle tribal economies from colonial controls, Congress passed the Indian Civil Rights Act of 1968 to guarantee the rights conferred by the US Bill of Rights to members of tribes and to require that tribal governments protect those rights. The act also amended P.L. 280 to require that states secure tribal approval before assuming civil and criminal jurisdiction over reservations.

In 1970, President Nixon explicitly repudiated tribal termination as a failure and changed the mission of US Indian policy to one of promoting tribal autonomy. That mission has been reinforced by subsequent presidents. Legislative and policy provisions under this self-determination umbrella include

- allowing tribes to take over administration of federal programs on their lands;
- rejecting assimilation in favor of recognizing tribes' permanent status as self-governing;
- increasing financial assistance to tribal governments;
- providing grants for tribes to operate their own schools;
- providing grants for tribal housing programs; and
- perhaps most importantly for building an attractive investment climate, giving tribes federal tax advantages enjoyed by state governments, including the power to issue tax-exempt bonds to finance public-sector projects.

The Confederated Salish & Kootenai Tribes (CSKT) on the Flathead Reservation in northwestern Montana are an example of what self-determination can do.[16] A study comparing tribal versus BIA management of forest resources on Indian reservations found that increased tribal control leads to higher worker productivity, reduces costs, and improves incomes.[17] Such evidence led Congress to allow some tribes to take greater control of their resources and tribal programs, starting with the Indian Self-Determination and Education Assistance Act of 1976 (Public Law 93-638). The CSKT took advantage of this opportunity by assuming authority over more than a hundred programs on their reservation. The upshot of this tribal control is summarized by researcher Alison Berry:

> Since the CSKT rely on timber revenues to support tribal operations, they have a vested interest in the continuing vitality of their natural resources. Tribal forest manager Jim Durglo comments, "Our forest is a vital part of everyday tribal life. Timber production, non-timber forest products, and grazing provide jobs and income for tribal members and enhance the economic life of surrounding communities." The tribes stand to benefit from responsible forest stewardship—or bear the burden of mismanagement.[18]

The Virtuous Circle of Investment

Even with the progress made so far toward self-determination, the barriers to economic growth erected by paternalistic policies remain such a formidable obstacle that very few outsiders want to do business in Indian Country. By raising the costs of investing, doing business, and creating capital, federal oversight has rendered tribal communities and reservations economic dead zones. Throughout Indian Country, leaders trying to revitalize tribal economies come face to face with the basic economic reality that investors have alternatives, and if the cost of doing business in Indian Country is too high, they will do business somewhere else. As Nancy Vermeulen, whose finance company in Billings, Montana, makes loans to Indians, explained to *Forbes* magazine, "We take on such a huge extra risk with someone from the reservation. If I knew contracts would be enforced, then I could do a lot more business there."[19] Without entrepreneurial investments to generate capital, growth in Indian Country is virtually impossible.

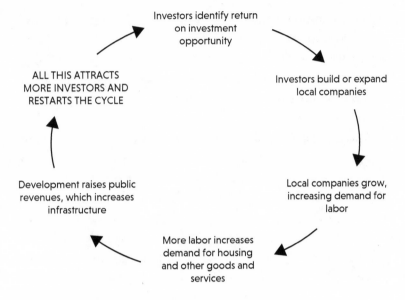

FIGURE 2.1. The Virtuous Circle

Source: Tulo Centre of Indigenous Economics, *Building a Competitive First Nation Investment Climate* (Kamloops, BC: Tulo Centre of Indigenous Economics, 2014), 40, https://www.tulo.ca.

Investment creates jobs; unleashes creative, artistic, and scientific potential within an economy; and encourages technological, organizational, and operational innovation. Investment also provides revenue for public investment in schools, libraries, roads, sewer, water systems, and social services. These are all part of the "virtuous circle," shown in figure 2.1.

Weaknesses in either the private- or public-sector components of the virtuous circle stymie economic renewal on reservations. Low investment means few employment opportunities and increases dependence on governments for basic services. Unemployment undermines individual and community self-sufficiency, and keeps tax revenue low. Lack of revenue limits the quantity and quality of infrastructure and of social services like education and health care, which, in turn, stymies the development of human capital.

This further erodes tribal integrity by creating strong incentives for individuals to seek opportunities outside the community or off the reservation. In Indian Country today the investment climate is fraught, and investment is inadequate to initiate or sustain the virtuous circle because of the high cost of doing business.

Assessing a potential investment anywhere begins with identifying and determining whether the costs of doing business are acceptable or, if not, whether they can be easily reduced to an acceptable level. Comparing the on- and off-reservation costs in a typical development project clarifies the heavier burden developers typically face when considering investments involving tribes or their members. The bottom line is that if the perceived costs, including opportunity and transaction costs, are higher than the expected benefits/capital gains from the project, investment will move elsewhere. That is why it is so difficult to attract investment to reservations and Indian communities.

Based on case studies of Canadian First Nations—whose development problems are similar to those of US tribes—the consulting firm Fiscal Realities applied transaction cost analysis to the seven steps of developing marketable property rights on Indian lands.[20] Table 2.1 describes each stage and compares on- and off-reservation cost.

These costs stem from institutional weakness, and their cumulative effect is to create an investment desert in Indian Country. Even the most risk-tolerant investors require some level of institutional certainty in property transactions, including

- established, stable land management rules and processes;
- land registry and tenure security;
- reliable recording;
- accurate, readily available demographic information; and
- a transparent system of taxation that reliably generates sufficient revenue to ensure public service and infrastructure quality.

TABLE 2.1. Development Stages and Transaction Costs

Stage	Description	Off-Reservation	On-Reservation
Project initiation/concept	Developer and/or community leaders identify suitable land and pitch the idea to the community. Includes initial due diligence and feasibility studies (economic & financial).	Able to research available real estate and approach local government development services office.	Little or no real estate information available and generally no development services office.
Land tenure certainty	Community creates land tenure certainty for the development.	Defined and managed through state and local legislation and bureaucracies (e.g., land-use planning and zoning).	Available only through BIA bureaucracy.
Land leasing	Land lease agreement is negotiated between developer and community.	Transactions usually facilitated by real estate industry and through state and local government titling agencies.	Subject to BIA requirements and approvals, often entailing additional cost.
Financing	Secure funding for the costs of development.	Financial industry is well-established and has experience with many financing models.	Little or no experience of financial industry.
Infrastructure development & services	Most significant projects require upgrading the existing physical infrastructure, building new infrastructure, and/or obtaining access to services and infrastructure in other jurisdictions.	Local governments provide many infrastructure-financing options and deliver local services.	Fewer financing options available; BIA policies and procedures are cumbersome, uncertain.
Legal framework for markets	Investors have certainty with respect to development costs and taxes, local service quality, local land-use, and other rules and laws, and recourse in the event of a dispute.	Investors have access, through state and local bureaucracies, to information about expected taxes, regulatory costs, investor recourse, and land-use regulations.	Much of this legal framework not clearly established; therefore, significant investor uncertainty.
Construction	Includes all the regulations associated with building standards, development approval processes, and risk, heritage, and environmental issues.	Building and engineering standards and bonded construction are common and readily available.	Building and engineering standards uncertainty and possible bonding issues.

Source: Adapted from Tulo Centre of Indigenous Economics, *Building a Competitive First Nation Investment Climate* (Kamloops, BC: Tulo Centre of Indigenous Economics, 2014), 49–50, https://www.tulo.ca.

All are problematic in tribal communities, making it harder for potential investors to analyze site suitability and project probable return on investment. The institutional weaknesses created by a century of colonization raise the costs of investment and perpetuate economic stagnation.

The effect of uncertainty on investment is readily apparent in the different amounts of energy resource development inside and outside reservation borders. Indian reservations contain almost 30 percent of America's coal reserves west of the Mississippi, 50 percent of America's potential uranium reserves, and 20 percent of America's known oil and gas reserves—resources worth nearly $1.5 trillion, or $290,000 per tribal member.[21] But, according to the US Department of the Interior, of the 15 million acres of potential energy and mineral resources on tribal lands, only 2.1 million acres are currently being developed.[22]

The Crow Reservation in Montana has coal assets valued at nearly $27 billion, making the tribe one of the largest coal owners in the world. Yet the tribe's annual rate of return on assets is a mere 0.01 percent, and it has reported unemployment rates as high as 78 percent.[23]

The Three Affiliated Tribes (Mandan, Hidatsa, and Arikara) of the Fort Berthold Reservation in North Dakota sit atop one of the nation's largest oil and gas plays, but twice as many wells have been drilled per square mile off-reservation as have been drilled on it.[24] As Marcus Levings, then chair of the Mandan, Hidatsa, and Arikara Nation, put it, "[Our] reservation looked like the hole of a donut. . . . Everything around us was moving, and there was nothing in the middle."[25] This hole stems partly from the fact that obtaining a permit to drill a well on the reservation requires developers to go through forty-nine steps and four federal agencies, compared to only four steps to drill off-reservation.[26]

Institutional Elements of Healthy Investment Climates

Renewed economies, like the economy of the Southern Ute Tribe, actively engage in the process of maintaining an institutional framework that supports market exchange. Of primary importance is establishing a healthy investment climate—which necessitates a supportive public sector. Investors need low-cost public services, infrastructure, and property-ownership certainty, which the public sector realizes through sound governance structures, regulations based on those structures, and effective adjudication and enforcement of public policies.

Chapter 1 documented the traditional institutions that allowed precontact Native Americans to thrive, not just survive. They had secure property rights, some of which were exclusive to individuals and some of which were collective. These property rights were enforced by well-established governance structures that provided some degree of certainty. Finally, traditional Indian economies encouraged trade within and between tribes and with European newcomers.

Colonialism undermined these traditional institutions and replaced them with top-down federal Indian laws that were inimical both to tribal customs and culture and to doing business in a modern economy. Market-supporting institutions are either missing or substandard in Indian Country today. The result is higher transaction costs of doing business on tribal lands than off them and, thus, insufficient investment to stimulate economic growth. Until these transaction costs are reduced, tribes will continue to receive less private investment, have less-developed economies, and experience below-average levels of health, education, and general well-being. The following chapters will examine, in turn, the property rights, governance and jurisdiction, and fiscal and financial frameworks necessary for contemporary tribes to renew their economies.

3

PROPERTY RIGHTS AND GOVERNANCE

The primary obstacle to economic development on American Indian reservations is the legacy of paternalistic rules that constrain ownership of reservation land and structures—privately or communally—and limit wealth-producing market exchange that depends on ownership. By restricting their ability to use and transfer property, the US government has for more than a century kept the benefits of specialization and trade beyond the reach of Indian people and communities.

The importance of property ownership to economic growth is difficult to overstate. In their comprehensive study *Why Nations Fail: The Origins of Power, Prosperity and Poverty*, economist Daron Acemoglu and political scientist James A. Robinson argue that secure property rights and the rule of law are the keys to understanding why some nation-states succeed and others fail.[1] American Indian nations are no exception.

While there are some issues like eminent domain and takings that can raise the costs of property transactions outside Indian Country, property markets generally work smoothly because owners have the right to determine the use and value of property. People owning property off reservations can rely on long-established procedures and protections, and can safely regard property transactions, such as buying or selling homes or leasing apartments or business space, as routine.

In Indian Country, on the other hand, "routine" property transactions are so rare as to be remarkable. The Urban Institute reports that land status remains a key structural barrier to mortgage lending and homeownership in tribal areas, despite some success in increasing lending. The homeownership rate among American Indians and Alaska Natives is growing, but still lags behind that of the general US population. Mortgage lending to the American Indian and Alaska Native (AIAN) population poses unique challenges. Because of land ownership arrangements in tribal areas, programs created to encourage mortgage lending have not been universally successful for AIAN populations.[2]

Even the Section 184 Loan Guarantees for Indian Housing program, which provides federal backing for housing loans, has had little success. Though the loan guarantee program was established to support tribal trust mortgage lending, the Department of Housing and Urban Development reports that "most (88 percent) Section 184 loans, however, were made for homes on fee simple land." This is because lenders find "daunting administrative barriers to establishing lease and title records. In addition, potential borrowers often have bad credit and lack knowledge of home buying and home ownership."[3] The bottom line is that property rights in Indian Country are incomplete because titles are not clear and because the federal government acts as trustee of millions of acres.

Property Rights—Nothing New under the Sun

As shown in chapter 1, tribes throughout the Americas had sophisticated private, communal, and usufruct systems of land rights long before Europeans introduced deeds and titling. Additional

examples include the Iroquois of southern Ontario, who organized themselves into bounded villages of about four hectares
surrounded by thirty-foot-high palisades and housing populations of two thousand.[4] The Acolhua-Aztec of central Mexico
demarcated the boundaries and calculated the areas of farms to
within a 10 percent error range for purposes of taxation and land
redistribution.[5] The Coast Salish peoples of the Pacific Northwest
recognized both individual and communal property rights.
Individuals and extended families held inheritable use rights to
small parcels such as root and clam beds, productive fishing spots,
and hunting ranges. Larger parcels, such as strips of coastline or
drainage basins, were held collectively by the community for hunting and fishing, and the territorial boundaries were defended.[6]

Indigenous oral histories are replete with references to individual and communal private property rights that, though they bore
little resemblance to European institutions of ownership, worked
quite well. As Michael Lebourdais, chair of the Tulo Centre of
Indigenous Economics, puts it,

> My people were part of the Canon and Fraser divisions of the
> Secwepemc. We were known as the greatest traders of our nation
> before contact. We traded with the Tsilhqot'in and other divisions of
> the Shuswap for profit. We understood markets and the institutions
> that support [them]. We had property rights for fishing sites and deer
> fences. We had inheritance rules to distribute the property of fathers
> among their children and closest relatives. We fought wars to protect
> our boundaries and property. Our elders have been seeking ownership
> of our lands since the 1870s. . . . We knew the value of our lands before
> contact and we continue to understand that value.[7]

Just as Europeans cannot be credited with introducing property
rights to the Americas, neither can they be charged with introducing conflict over property. Territory was the basis for wars between

tribes before contact and continued to be a source of intertribal conflict throughout the nineteenth century and into the reservation period. As Hämäläinen notes in his comprehensive history of the Lakota, "Sioux went to war for complex reasons—to protect their lands, to exact revenge, to secure hunting and trading privileges, to enhance their power and prestige by taking slaves, to preempt threats—and the threshold for a military campaign was low."[8]

The level of conflict and devastation rose dramatically when White settlers entered the fray. Backed by the US Army, the settlers prevailed. Millions of acres of land were transferred to White ownership and tribes were confined on reservations much smaller than their traditional homelands. It is important to note, however, that even on reservations, tribes established and maintained informal but nonetheless sophisticated property rights institutions. The once-roaming Blackfeet, for example, established a complex system that incorporated both communal rights to grazing land and private individual rights to the cattle grazing on the communal land.

The Indian Wars ended by the 1890s, but the process of dispossession continued through policy and regulation. Indian peoples have long asserted that they did not willingly transfer their rights in return for protective guardianship that they neither asked for nor wanted. In the words of Chief Joseph, revered Nez Perce chief:

> If we ever owned the land we own it still, for we never sold it. In the treaty councils the commissioners have claimed that our country had been sold to the government. Suppose a white man should come to me and say, Joseph, I like your horses, and I want to buy them. Then he goes to my neighbor and says to him; Joseph's horses. I want to buy them but he refuses to sell. My neighbor answers, pay me the money and I will sell you Joseph's horses. The white man returns to me, and says, Joseph, I have bought your horses and you must let me have them. If we sold our lands to the government, this is the way they were bought.[9]

Asserting as they did that Native Americans were "wards" of the federal government, as discussed in chapter 2, paternalistic Indian policies ignored the historical success of Indigenous institutions, placed all Indian land in trust, and appointed Congress and the Department of the Interior as protective trustees. The dismal record of federal management of these lands is an issue in its own right, but it should not overshadow the more fundamental question of whether the ongoing governmental paternalism has been or is in any way beneficial or just arrogantly demeaning.

> Almost every community is located on a . . . tract of land—usually the size of a postage-stamp—set aside by the federal government for specific bands of Indian people. No one particular Indian person "owns" the land; it is held by the [government] for the collective benefit of everyone in the Indian band. The notion that [Indian] lands, which we have occupied since before contact, must now be held by the government on our behalf is . . . bizarre.[10]

The rest of this chapter explains how strong property-rights institutions sustain markets and incentivize economic growth, and then provides examples of the problems tribes face today under the weakened property rights imposed by federal policy.

People Make Property Valuable

Formally institutionalized property rights are ubiquitous outside Indian Country. They exist for tangible objects such as cars, furniture, land, and livestock, and for intangible, intellectual possessions like ideas, symbols, writings, music, and data. They are the bedrock of exchange. When consumers purchase goods and services, they trade income (or in some cases, future income) for ownership and control of property. As the result of the "virtuous circle" (see chapter 2), property rights facilitate win-win voluntary exchanges that result in continuous economic growth for society.

Even if owners imbue land with great spiritual or cultural significance, as is the case of many societies, including those of Native Americans, it is important to recognize that in and of itself land has no rights; only human beings do. Ownership rights are fundamentally human rights—institutional rules of the game about what owners and nonowners can and cannot do vis-à-vis other human beings and their rights. Establishing rights to property evokes the necessity of enforcing those rights, either through customs and culture or by governing authorities.

The Components of Property Rights

Lawyers and economists often portray property rights as a bundle of sticks. The sticks are the provisions of use defined by customs, culture, administrative systems, and legal codes. Property-rights bundles include permissions and restrictions, both of which are necessary for exchange and economic growth. For example, the buyer of a music-streaming application purchases the right to listen to music on her phone or tablet, but not the right to record and sell it. This set of privileges and constraints allows consumers to derive value and preserves producers' incentive to supply music.

The principal "sticks" in the property rights "bundle" fall into three main categories:

- *Use*—the right to enjoy and/or derive profit from the property
- *Exclusion*—the right to deny use of the property to others
- *Disposition*—the right to transfer or dispose of the property[11]

The strength of each stick in the bundle depends on how it is formally and informally limited.

Use, or usufruct, rights range from the simple (as with the right of an individual owner to live on her land and to construct buildings or plant crops) to the complex (as when a few or many owners are empowered to make management decisions about a property). The right to use may or may not be paired with the right to exclude. A condominium owner, for example, may use the clubhouse and swimming pool, but may not lock the gate to exclude other owners. Use can also be a partial right, as in the case of fishing club members who can catch fish, but have no right to the water, the streambed, or the surrounding property. While owners commonly derive immediate benefits, their use rights may also generate future, unknowable benefits, like the dividends distributed to stockholders.

Exclusion covers owners' rights to allow or deny the benefits of their property to others. The right to exclude is always qualified by the government's power to ensure that owners exercise their rights in ways that do not harm others or violate their rights. For example, a rancher can exclude neighbors from grazing cattle on his land, but cannot stop a municipality with the power of eminent domain from taking a corner of his ranch to widen a public road. A beachfront homeowner may exclude people from all of her beach in some states, but only from the area above the high-tide line in others.

Disposition is the power to transfer property to others, either permanently by sale, gift, or inheritance, or temporarily by leasing or renting. Like other sticks in the property-rights bundle, the right to dispose of property is limited by law and regulation. The purchaser of a candy bar owns the wrapper, but may not legally dispose of it out the car window. The owner of a farm with a stream running through it may sell the farm, but not the water.

All three components of property rights are present and enforceable in fee simple ownership, the strongest form of land ownership and the most common form outside Indian Country. Landowners with fee simple title enjoy a large measure of confidence that their rights are clearly defined and protected. Limitations on fee simple ownership do exist—the prohibition against knowingly renting property for criminal activity, for example—but they are generally regarded as necessary for the public good and are not so onerous as to stifle economic activity.

Individually and in their tribal communities, Native Americans are systematically denied the benefits of these three components of property ownership. Their ability to use, transfer, and exclude others is restricted by the federal trustee of their land. The trustee's regulatory and administrative rules curtail development by disallowing the use of land as collateral for loans. The prohibitive cost of completing transactions on even the best-located tribal lands effectively blocks investment and entrepreneurship.

This can be understood in the context of individual trust lands on reservations. Driving through a western reservation provides a picture of how trusteeship—incomplete property rights—reduces productivity and wealth creation. A 160-acre parcel that is overgrazed and a house that is not well maintained did not get that way because the Native American "owners" were ignorant of the value of taking care of assets, but because the "owners" have very few sticks in the bundle of rights. He or she has limited use of the land, mainly for occupancy and grazing; he or she can exclude others from grazing, but not from hunting; and he or she cannot transfer sticks in the bundle to others, except temporarily, and then only with permission from the BIA. In contrast, when you see irrigated land in cultivation, well-maintained farm implements, and a barn and well-kept house, you can be sure the "owner" of the land, whether an Indian or a non-Indian, holds it in fee simple, with the bundle of sticks for use, exclusion, and exchange confidently in hand.

Property Rights and Law in Indian Country

The bundle of property-rights sticks held by Native Americans prior to European contact was created by tribal culture and norms, but since the creation of reservations, most sticks in the bundle have been held by the federal government. The policies that regulate everything from Indians' land use to their ability to make decisions about their own mental and physical health are determined in Washington, DC, by the Department of the Interior through the BIA and the Bureau of Indian Education, and by the Department of Health and Human Services through the Indian Health Service.

The area of jurisdiction known as Indian Country, to which Indian policy applies, is defined by the United States federal criminal code (18 US Code § 1151) as

- land within the boundaries of an Indian reservation, including rights-of-way through a reservation;
- dependent Indian communities within the borders of the United States; and
- all individual Indian allotments, including rights-of-way, and excluding allotments for which Indian title has been extinguished.[12]

Real property in Indian Country may be owned in fee simple by either Indians or non-Indians, but is mostly held in trust for both individuals and tribes by the federal government. It is trusteeship that removes so many sticks from tribes' and individual Indians' bundles of rights. The lands for which the federal government acts as trustee do have individual or group names attached to them, but the principal components of property rights discussed above are lacking. The result is three very distinct categories of landownership:

- *Unrestricted fee simple land.* Unrestricted title is held by the tribe, tribal members, or non–tribal members.
- *Tribal trust land.* The tribe is the legal beneficiary, but title is held by the federal government.

- *Individual trust land.* The individual Indian retains a beneficial interest in the land, but legal title is held by the federal
government. Under trusteeship, individuals may hold the use
and exclusion "sticks" in the property-rights bundle but not
the right to transfer title to others.

Of the over 50 million acres of land in Indian Country under the
jurisdiction of the BIA, approximately 75 percent is held in tribal
trust, 20 percent is held in individual trusts, and only 5 percent is
held in fee simple.[13] The 75 percent tribal trust portion of reservation land is, in economic and legal parlance, *collective* property held
communally, meaning that the tribe, as a single legal entity, owns the
undivided beneficial interest in the land, and through its representatives (usually a tribal council) it controls use of the land for the benefit of tribal members. This arrangement is intended to protect the
tribal land base by establishing continuity of beneficial ownership.

Theoretically, the tribe's collective property could be held as
a shared *commons* with no member having a claim to any specific location or piece of land. In practice, however, people dis-
like the uncertainties and conflict that often arise in communal
ownership when more than a few are involved, so many tribes
use *assignments* to divide the interests. Assignments give individuals explicit permissions to use specific parcels of land in
designated ways such as demarcating them for grazing cattle or
setting up a cigarette or fireworks stand, or building a house. "The
terms of assignments may vary greatly in duration and scope.
They often expire after a term of years without any guaranteed
right of renewal, and they usually are personal to the assignee. . . .
However, there is a pronounced tendency to renew an assignment
once given and permit descendants to acquire the assignment of
a deceased assignee."[14] Even on reservations using assignments,
land ownership is still *collective*, meaning that transferring an
assignment requires consent either from every individual tribal

member or from a tribal government with the legal status to represent all the members.

Investors naturally prefer the simplicity of negotiating with a representative of the tribe as a single owner rather than dealing with multiple individuals or with the tribes' internal decision-making procedures. In theory, assignments should streamline exchange, but in practice, the behind-the-scenes workings of tribal decision making are often drawn out and may be a source of ongoing friction within a tribe and of uncertainty or costly delays to investors. When more than one tribe occupies a reservation or claims the same property, the problems and accompanying costs increase even more, as different tribes have different cultures and different objectives.[15]

Economists refer to the costs of achieving agreements about land use and land exchange as the costs of doing business or simply as transaction costs. As transaction costs increase with collective ownership and multiple decision makers, they can exceed the value of taking actions that would increase land productivity and land values. This can mean that "owners" receive less income from using the land to generate revenue or derive less subjective value from restricting land use to achieve cultural and religious ends.

Trusteeship increases transaction costs to investors dealing with tribes in multiple ways:

- The collective (BIA or tribe) holds the underlying title but has not transferred all of the sticks in the property-rights bundle to the individual who occupies the property in question.
- The trust relationship obligates the federal government to ensure that collective property is used for the benefit of all tribal members, so exchanges require bureaucratic approvals.
- Jurisdictional and regulatory squabbles with state and local governments emerge because collective ownership has been poorly defined.

In addition to high transaction costs of exchange, business dealings involving collective property for which multiple decision makers share authority face two incentive problems. The first is the free-riding problem, the incentive for an owner to let other owners bear the cost of any improvements designed to increase benefits. The second is the holding-out problem, which occurs when any single owner has the ability to prevent a beneficial transaction from occurring by withholding permission unless he or she gets a larger share of the gains. Both of these problems are exacerbated as the number of owners increases.

Shrinking Indian Country through Allotment and Termination

From the beginning of the reservation period, government policy bounced back and forth between segregating Indians from the larger population and forcing them to assimilate into the American melting pot. By the 1880s, most Indians were effectively segregated on tribal reservations, and most reservation land was tribal trust land.

The 25 percent of Indian land that is held in individual trust or in fee simple title traces back to the General Allotment Act, also called the Dawes Act, of 1887. The Indian Land Tenure Foundation estimates that over ninety million acres were lost, including sixty million acres sold as "surplus" that was not "needed" for allotments.[16]

Public policy swung back to promoting segregation with the passage of the Indian Reorganization Act (IRA, or Wheeler Howard Act) in 1934. Intended to establish reservations as permanent, protected Indian homelands, the IRA ended allotment and put into permanent individual trust any allotted parcels for which the temporary trust period had not expired. These became the individual trust lands found on many reservations today. Tribal governments have no authority to direct the use of individual trust parcels on reservations, and owners' decisions about use of the property are subject to federal government approval.

> The legal title to most existing allotments is held by the United States, with the entire beneficial interest being in the individual allottees. Some allottees were issued patents in fee, however, with a restraint on alienation. The two types of allotments [restricted and unrestricted] are treated identically. Decisions concerning the use or disposition of such land accordingly must be made by the allottees, not the tribe, with the concurrence of the United States. The United States as trustee is not entitled to deal informally with a mortgage creditor and seize and lease allotted land without the participation of the allottee.[17]

Beyond massive land loss, allotment created other conditions that hinder development, one of which, fractionation, makes land-use decisions intractable. Fractionation occurs when heirship rules require land to be willed to multiple heirs. Although individual allottees were allowed to will their parcels to heirs as they saw fit, most Indians died intestate, meaning that succession of the beneficial interest in the land was determined by the state in which the allotment was located. Many states simply required that the land be allocated in equal shares to all heirs. As a result, each heir received an undivided share in the land, and the number of shareholders increased exponentially as the share was passed on. The result, predictable in hindsight, is dozens, hundreds, and even thousands of owners with an undivided interest in the land. According to the Indian Land Tenure Foundation, "This makes it nearly impossible for any one of the owners to use the land for agriculture, business development or a home site."[18]

Figure 3.1 illustrates how fractionation occurs.

Checkerboarding is another result of allotment that seriously impairs the ability of tribes or individual members to use land for

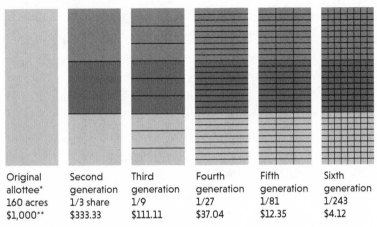

Original allottee* 160 acres $1,000**	Second generation 1/3 share $333.33	Third generation 1/9 $111.11	Fourth generation 1/27 $37.04	Fifth generation 1/81 $12.35	Sixth generation 1/243 $4.12

*Presumes three heirs per person per generation.
**Hypothetical amount an interest holder might earn from their share of the property.

FIGURE 3.1. A Simplified Six-Generation Example of Fractionation
Source: Indian Land Tenure Foundation, https://iltf.org.

farming, ranching, or other economic activities that require large, contiguous parcels. Checkerboarding is created by the combination of fee simple, individual trust, and tribal trust lands in no apparent pattern. Figure 3.2 illustrates the complex mosaic on one reservation.

Costly jurisdictional challenges are common on checkerboard reservations as different governing authorities—including county, state, federal, and tribal governments—claim the authority to regulate, tax, or perform various activities within reservation borders. Often these different claims to authority conflict, resulting in economic uncertainty, racial tension, and community clashes within or near the reservation. To complicate matters, the case law relevant to jurisdiction on Indian land is highly complex and, on some points, inconsistent and unsettled.[19]

Allotments ended in 1953, and House Resolution 108 (83rd Cong., 1st Sess.; 67 Stat. B132) initiated what became known as termination, a policy name that would prove to be sadly predictive for

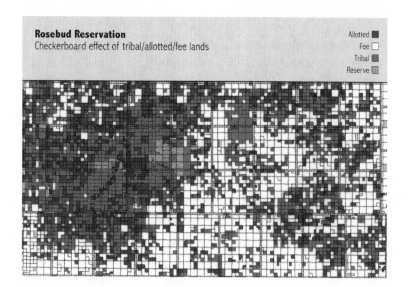

FIGURE 3.2. Example of Checkerboarding
Source: Indian Land Tenure Foundation, https://iltf.org.

tribes and for their individual members. The policy was intended to terminate tribal structures "as rapidly as possible to make the Indians within the territorial limits of the United States subject to the same laws and entitled to the same privileges and responsibilities as are applicable to other citizens of the United States, [and] to end their status as wards of the United States."[20]

Although it was designed by reformers to free Indians from the grasp of the BIA, termination was one more instance in which intentions did not lead to positive outcomes for Indians. In human terms, the termination of 109 mainly West Coast tribes can be regarded as nothing short of disastrous. Ill-prepared for urban life and lacking the skills needed to succeed in an industrializing economy, thousands of Indians ended up more impoverished in cities than they had been on their reservations.[21]

The effects of termination were exacerbated by a concurrent relocation program. To address the high unemployment on reservations, the BIA offered cash grants to individuals willing to move to designated urban centers where, they were assured, they would find meaningful and dependable employment. Most did not. Their grants quickly dwindled, and they joined the ranks of the urban poor, stripped of meaningful identity and of the support of their cultural institutions.

The Coushatta Indian Tribe of Louisiana was terminated in 1953 without their consent or specific legislation; the federal government simply stopped making available to them federal funding for services like health care and education. It took twenty years for the tribe to win back its status as a sovereign nation with the right to deal one-on-one, government to government, with the United States. It is ironic that this terminated tribe was required to purchase land in order to regain federal recognition of its sovereign status. In 1973, the federal government designated fifteen contiguous acres in south-west Louisiana near the town of Elton as the Coushatta Reservation. The tribe has since increased its holdings by more than six thousand acres.[22]

President Richard Nixon repudiated termination in 1970, calling it a failure and initiating a new policy of self-determination for Indian nations. By that time over 1,365,000 acres of land had been removed from trust status and more than thirteen thousand people had lost affiliation with their tribes.

Property Rights and Investment Climates

The reservation property-rights system was never intended to support economic growth. Fee simple property rights were not granted to tribes or individuals because Indians were not considered responsible enough to use reservation land in their best interest. Rather, the intent of holding land in trust was to maintain the federal government as the trustee in order to protect Native Americans as wards of the state. As a result, no land registry system was created like those typical in counties across the United States that facilitate transactions and provide security to potential investors.[23] Instead, recordation of Indian trust lands is done by the Division of Land Titles and Records, which maintains eighteen Land Titles and Records Offices, leaving trust lands entangled in a bureaucratic morass. Indian nations thus entered the era of self-determination burdened by a climate that stifled internal economic initiative and discouraged outside investment (see chapter 4).

In *The Mystery of Capital*, Peruvian economist Hernando de Soto argues that weak property rights create unhealthy investment climates because property becomes "dead capital" that cannot be used to finance additional capital construction. De Soto identifies six elements of healthy investment climates that provide the institutional assurances investors have come to expect. As summarized in table 3.1, the absence or weakness of these elements in Indian economies as a result of cumbersome property-rights institutions heightens risk, increases uncertainty, and deters investment.[24]

- *Reliable asset evaluation and appraisal.* Strong property-rights systems facilitate transactions by making property values clear. The market value of a home, for example, is a key component of an equity loan agreement and therefore one of the first pieces of information a lender requires. While value appraisal is a routine task outside Indian Country, the market value of many assets on reservations is difficult, if not impossible, to determine.
- *Integration of dispersed information.* Property-rights registry systems that provide information about use and ownership facilitate asset evaluations and exchanges. Registries and measurement records certify information about a property's attributes, significantly reducing the cost of comparing assets. Registration and measurement are difficult to accomplish on Indian lands, in part because the information is so widely dispersed.

- *Accountability.* Well-defined property rights facilitate contracts between strangers by establishing that each party has something to lose by not adhering to the agreement. Contracts create legally binding, enforceable commitments that protect the parties involved and generate trust. Under a contract, those who do not pay for goods or services they have consumed can be identified, charged interest penalties, fined, embargoed, or have their credit ratings downgraded. The investment climate is strengthened by accountability, which has proven difficult for tribal governments to establish.
- *Fungible assets.* Sound property-rights administrative systems allow assets to be adapted, split up, or combined for use in different economic circumstances. Most Indian property is not fungible because it is held in trust; this increases the risk to investors because they cannot use the land as collateral for loans.
- *Networking.* Stable, reliable land-registry systems not only provide information important to exchange, but they also establish networks in which property can be confidently identified and tracked. A strong system of protection for property rights facilitates networking among citizens, governments, and private-sector business interests. Such networks simplify the provision and maintenance of utilities and the bill collection that funds them.[25] Distance and isolation on the biggest reservations make internal networking unproductive at best and networking with off-reservation businesses unlikely.
- *Transaction protection.* Modern property-rights systems make transactions for large and small assets secure, a necessary condition for investor certainty. The abrupt jurisdictional change that occurs at reservation boundaries and the lack of secure transactions legislation on most reservations are continuing sources of uncertainty and serve as major deterrents to potential off-reservation investors and partners.

TABLE 3.1. Weak Indian Property Rights

Investment Climate Attributes	Status in Indian Country
Asset evaluation	Land and property value difficult to determine; assessed value difficult to access or not available.
Information integration	Property records not integrated with other information common in nonreservation systems; survey information often unavailable.
Accountability	Trust status prevents use of property as collateral in loans; many loans require third-party guarantees.
Asset fungibility	Property assets difficult to combine owing to poor information integration, missing accountability, etc.; more difficult to assess tribal government credit.
Networking	Property information not networked into many other systems; utilities often missing or substandard.
Transaction protection	Few examples of individual property combined with other properties for significant investments.

Source: Adapted from Tulo Centre of Indigenous Economics, *Building a Competitive First Nation Investment Climate* (Kamloops, BC: Tulo Centre of Indigenous Economics, 2014), 88, https://www.tulo.ca.

These elements are routinely missing or weak in Indian Country land tenure.

The deficiencies in Indian property-rights institutions have both immediate and long-term consequences for investment, whether the property is owned by individuals; by groups such as partnerships, trusts, or corporations; or by communities such as tribes or municipalities. The existing property-rights framework does not attract off-reservation investors, provide secure and tradable individual property rights that allow members to access capital, incorporate regulations sufficient to provide investor certainty, or integrate information through a modern registry to reduce transaction costs.

Addressing Property-Rights Issues

Under self-determination, Congress has taken steps to strengthen tribal property rights. The Indian Land Consolidation Act of 1983 initiated a pilot land purchase program (subsequently amended and then made permanent in 2014) to address checkerboarding and fractionation. "The Amendments authorized the Secretary of the Interior to acquire from willing sellers, and at fair market value, any fractional interest in trust or restricted land, to: Prevent further fractionation; consolidate fractional interests and ownership into usable parcels in the name of the Tribe/Band in a manner that enhances tribal sovereignty; promote tribal self-sufficiency and self-determination; and to reverse the effects of the allotment policy on Indian Tribes."[26]

Additional legislation to strengthen Indian property rights includes the following:

- *Contracts with Indians.* This 2000 amendment to 25 U.S.C.A. § 81 eliminated the statutory requirement, in effect since the beginning of the reservation period, that the Secretary of the Interior must approve all tribal land-use contracts. The amended act requires approval only for contracts that encumbered Indian land for seven or more years.
- *HEARTH Act.* The HEARTH (Helping Expedite and Advance Responsible Tribal Homeownership) Act of 2012 allowed tribes to lease land for up to twenty-five years for residential, business, public, religious, educational, or recreational uses without the approval of the Secretary of the Interior, while maintaining exemption from state and local taxation.
- *Land Buy-Back Program for Tribal Nations.* Initiated in 2012, this program consolidates tribal lands by purchasing non-Indian-owned parcels in checkerboards using funds from the settlement of *Cobell v. Salazar*, a class-action suit brought against the federal government for mismanaging trust funds. The 2009 settlement included $1.9 billion to consolidate fractional interests in trust or restricted land from 2012 through November 2022. In 2019, the Department of the Interior

sent more than $2 million in offers from the Land Buy-Back Program to nearly 1,600 landowners with fractional interests in land on the Santee Sioux Reservation in Nebraska.[27]

Conclusion

Despite the challenges and roadblocks, Indian governments can take meaningful steps to establish market-oriented property-rights systems. Although tribes' circumstances, and therefore their needs, differ, some general guidelines for this effort are applicable to all.

- *The larger the market for individual property rights, the higher their value.* Options that can possibly or significantly increase the market size for property are superior to those that cannot.
- *Locations closer to markets and resources are superior to locations farther away.* Investment can reduce the real or virtual distance to markets and raise the value of property.
- *A modern land-registry system improves the investment climate.* Without a land-registry system based on more precise coordinates, like those used by states and counties, and with documents easily retrievable at courthouses or tribal offices, it is difficult for tribes or individuals with trust land to use their assets to back investments. Making land available for loan collateral is necessary to increasing capital investment on reservations.
- *A regulatory framework to support property rights that minimizes transaction costs is superior to one that does not.* It is uncertain whether tribes will be successful in lowering transaction costs if they develop their own unique legal frameworks, so it is important for them to consider adopting or integrating existing options that have been developed via legislation or regulation or established through the courts. Regulatory options that are faster or cheaper to implement are

preferable to those that are slower and more costly. Uniform Commercial Codes supported by reliable judicial systems are an example of existing legal frameworks that can lower transaction costs. The more of the legal framework that the tribe has to develop and implement itself, the more expensive and slower the option.

Indian tribes throughout the North American continent had collective and individual property-rights systems long before contact. In the United States, those institutions and the economic benefits they created were legislated away during the late nineteenth and early twentieth centuries. A haphazard series of policies administered by the BIA relegated Indians to wardship status with little to no ability to leverage their property for investment in capital. The cumulative effect of federal Indian policy has been to entrench a property-rights system that provides no regulatory certainty, a land-registry system that is slow and cumbersome, and individual and tribal property rights that are mostly not marketable. Together these conditions perpetuate poor investment climates with high transaction costs, low property values, and poor access to capital.

Under the policy of self-determination, the common objectives are (1) to restore tribal and individual property rights on par with those of non-Indian Americans, and (2) to construct legal frameworks that support marketable property rights and facilitate investment. The next chapter examines the role of jurisdiction and governance institutions in achieving that second objective.

4

CREATING A POSITIVE INVESTMENT CLIMATE

Traditional Indigenous economies in North America were no strangers to capital accumulation and investment. The mound earthworks constructed by Mississippian peoples, the cliff dwellings of the Anasazi, and the miles of stone walls used to drive buffalo over piskuns on the Plains required considerable investment in anticipation of returns over a long period. To incentivize those who made the investments (individuals or groups), ownership claims would have had to be sufficiently strong to ensure that they would reap a return on their efforts.

To make investments, people had to have a surplus above subsistence, which could then be saved for the creation of capital. Only with a surplus above subsistence can individuals or groups choose not to consume some of their production. The surplus might be food that can be used to feed those building a mound or cliff dwelling. As Charles Mann explained in his book *1491*, "Building a ring of mounds with baskets or deerskins full of dirt is a long-term enterprise. During construction the workers must eat, which in turn means that other people must provide their food."[1]

The same applies to the clam gardens along the Pacific Northwest coast, of which two thousand have been identified. To increase clam production, clans sometimes built boulder walls by rolling huge rocks onto the beach. The walls, which required continued maintenance as the tides moved them around, trapped sediment into which clam "seeds" (larvae) were planted for later harvest. This intensive mariculture could not have happened without savings (surplus production) and secure ownership claims.

The climate that encouraged investment in traditional Indigenous economies is the same climate necessary for tribes who would renew their economies today. They must create transparent, dependable legal frameworks that encourage savings, ensure security to investors by protecting property rights, and reduce the costs of doing business. Weak or absent investment institutions discourage investment and entrench poverty.

This chapter explains how tribal law relates to tribal investment climates by identifying the components of legal frameworks that support investment and the gaps in legal frameworks that impede it. It also examines issues of tribal sovereign immunity, trusteeship, and jurisdictional uncertainty that weaken tribal investment climates; insecurities in credit markets that stifle investment; and the potential for the Model Tribal Secured Transactions Act to fill some gaps in tribal legal frameworks through cost-reducing standardization.

Investor Assessment of the Business Climate

Suppose an investor is considering two identical projects for a commitment of capital—one on tribal land and one off. Further, suppose the price is the same. How would he or she choose? Regardless of the type or size of the business, be it a small commercial enterprise or a large venture, investors evaluate opportunities by estimating their potential rates of return.

A number of factors influence the potential rate of return; some factors are of fundamental concern across all types of investment options, and others are specific to the particular legal environment of an individual project. Investors routinely begin their assessments by seeking answers to three broad questions about the existing legal rules and governmental institutions within which they must operate. Here are several questions they ask.

1. *What are the property laws?* Formal laws as well as customs and culture define ownership claims and outline the extent to which governments can interfere with owners' use. As we saw in chapter 3, laws that reduce uncertainty about future costs, processes, and services encourage investment. A legal framework that protects ownership claims and creates transparent processes respecting property uses creates certainty and strengthens investor confidence, thereby increasing the rate of return. Governments' powers over property can be extensive, including but not limited to expropriation, seizure (for unpaid taxes), or zoning restrictions. All or any of these government powers can significantly affect—negatively or positively—property values, the cost of doing business, and the ability to estimate future rates of return.

2. *Are property rights strong, weak, or absent?* When personal property rights are strong, owners have an incentive to husband and make investments to improve their assets; when they are weak or absent, wealth-creating markets languish. Exchange depends on parties having clear ownership of whatever they sell.

3. *What are the availability and quality of public services and infrastructure?* Public infrastructure supports investment, as does a legal framework to ensure such services are adequately provided and maintained. Investors' estimates of rates of return are based partly on expectations that some public services such as roads, water, sewer, and law enforcement (to mention a few) will be provided by the government. If services and infrastructure are available, investors need to know that

the legal framework ensures their long-term provision and maintenance. If services and infrastructure are not available, investors will ask whether the existing legal framework will provide for them in the future, and if so, at what cost in taxes and fees to the investor. Investors must have confidence in the processes that determine security of property rights and delivery of public services.

4. *What are the regulations and methods of recourse?* Regulations specify the procedures for doing business within a governmental jurisdiction and the methods of recourse when there are disputes over regulations. Investors want to know the rules of the game and the players who take the field during the entire process, from planning to completion to operation. Who are the decision makers? How are decisions made? What is the timeline for decisions? Clear and transparent rules of the game help investors to accurately assess costs and estimate rates of return. Investors also want to know that they have recourse if there are disputes over the rules. Are reasons given for decisions? Is there an appeal process? Is the appeal process fair?

In investment-friendly reservation climates, the answers to these questions reassure investors that the costs of doing business are transparent and that processes for all aspects of development, from planning through completion and operation, are fair and efficient. Incomplete or unclear processes, on the other hand, increase investors' fears that projects will not be approved, that costs cannot be reliably estimated, or that costs will increase because of administrative delays.

Governments Shape Investment Climates

The legal frameworks governments establish affect business costs, both directly through tax laws and policies and indirectly through the administrative processes and procedures required for development. Directly, governments can lower costs to specific businesses through tax policy, or favor one industry or business over another in how tax revenue is spent. Examples include installing specialized infrastructure or offering tax breaks in order to attract a particular developer.

Indirectly, a tribe's legal framework supports and encourages investment when it increases certainty, lowers the costs of doing business, and supports the tribe's existing or developing comparative advantage. Rules must be clear and transparent and be applied consistently to all investors. Laws that establish property rights, delineate governmental powers, enforce contractual terms, and clearly outline approval requirements increase investors' ability to assess costs, risks, and timelines and increase their confidence that the system will support their investment now and in the future. Logically, it is also the case that poorly constructed laws, or no laws, undermine certainty and deter investment.

Governments can lower transaction costs by adopting standardized procedures that have proven to be both transparent and efficient. In the event that standardized rules of the game are missing or unfamiliar, transaction costs rise significantly because the law and policies must either be developed by the jurisdictional authority or captured in contracts negotiated on a case-by-case basis—both costly, time-consuming alternatives. Laws that adopt processes widely used across jurisdictions also lower transaction costs because investors do not need to learn new systems.

Consider the message to a prospective developer when a jurisdiction can point to a long-standing record of stable, timely, nonpoliticized administration, or well-maintained roads, or reliable internet access. Or, on the flip side, consider the message if the institutional infrastructure shows a history of instability, with destructive political infighting and frequent, unpredictable changes in policies and procedures. Tribal governments with established positive records for

lowering transaction costs and providing stable political environments are the exception rather than the rule. Potential investors
routinely discover big gaps in the legal framework of business support in Indian Country.

Constitutional and Judicial Definition of Tribes' Legal Status

As discussed in chapter 2, the legal gaps in reservation investment
climates can be traced to the Constitution and to early Supreme
Court decisions that established the legal status of reservations
and the federal and state divisions of powers over tribal lands
(federalism). After the American Revolution, the states were either
unable or unwilling to stop the cycle of citizen aggression and Indian
retaliation, so the Articles of Confederation, the precursor to the
Constitution, placed control over Indian affairs with the federal
government. In a de facto acknowledgment of the sovereign-
nation status of Indian tribes, Congress and the president were
given exclusive power to regulate commerce and make treaties
with tribes. Federal control over Indian affairs was maintained in
the drafting of the Constitution and consolidated in the Trade and
Intercourse Acts of 1790 and 1834.

The basis for all Indian policy and legislation up to and including
the present day is found in Supreme Court decisions that date from
the earliest years of the republic in response to conflicts between
Indian tribes and land-hungry colonists and, later, between state
and federal jurisdictions. Legal scholar William C. Canby Jr. calls
Cherokee Nation v. Georgia (1831) and *Worcester v. Georgia* (1832),
both of which were part of the Marshall Trilogy (see chapter 2),
"the two most influential decisions in all of Indian law."[2] These cases
arose from the Georgia state government's attempts to nullify all
Cherokee title within state boundaries. As discussed in chapter 2,

the decision in *Cherokee Nation* denied Georgia and affirmed the status of the tribe as a nation-state capable of self-government. Together, these cases lay the foundation for Indian tribes' legal status as sovereign nation-states and individual Indians' status as wards of the federal government. States have not quietly acquiesced to their hands-off status, and many cases in the ensuing centuries tested the limits of state power to tax, regulate, and adjudicate the Indian citizens and reservations within their boundaries. For the most part, the Supreme Court, while noting the absence of clarifying congressional legislation, has deferred to the sovereignty of Indian nations established by treaty, but challenges by state and local governments continue.

Most recently, the state of Oklahoma asserted its power to try an accused rapist despite the crime having occurred on lands given to the Muscogee (Creek) Nation when they were removed from Georgia by President Andrew Jackson. Oklahoma claimed jurisdiction in the original 1996 trial, arguing that the enabling legislation creating the state in 1906 had "disestablished" the reservations created at the time the tribes were removed from Georgia. The accused, Jimcy McGirt, appealed his conviction, and the case eventually reached the Supreme Court. The decision in *McGirt v. Oklahoma*, written by Justice Neil Gorsuch and issued July 9, 2020, denied the state's claim and affirmed what Justice Gorsuch called the promise at the end of the Trail of Tears. In what has been heralded throughout Indian Country as a victory for tribal sovereignty, he wrote,

Under our Constitution, States have no authority to reduce federal reservations lying within their borders. Just imagine if they did. A State could encroach on the tribal boundaries or legal rights Congress provided, and, with enough time and patience, nullify the promises made in the name of the United States. That would be at odds with the Constitution, which entrusts Congress with the authority to regulate commerce with Native Americans, and directs that federal treaties and statutes are the "supreme Law of the Land."[3]

In *McGirt*, the Court established that the Muscogee (Creek) Nation is a sovereign government and has judicial jurisdiction over its territory. This case is extremely important for establishing tribal jurisdiction and tribal sovereignty. Despite the ruling, however (and with a few notable exceptions), tribes today exercise little authority in most spheres of government responsibility, including courts, police, taxation, and zoning, to mention a few. Hence, they are sovereign nations in name alone.

Even when tribes obtain some jurisdictional authority, as with *McGirt*, a practical consequence of Indians' ward status is to weaken the investment climate and slow development by subjecting all exchanges with Indian individuals or tribes to third-party approval. The title to all reservation land and most allotments is held by the federal government, which, as trustee, is responsible for ensuring that the land and resources are used for the benefit of the tribes and individual allottees. The BIA oversees and administers the trust and must approve all resource usage agreements and transactions, including leases, subleases, and amendments for development projects and mortgages for individuals. Additionally, as sovereign states, Indian nations are immune from suit and are preempted from encumbrance and taxation, increasing investor uncertainty about recourse and confusing the question of jurisdiction should disputes arise. Three questions capture such uncertainties:

- What are the privileges and limitations of tribal sovereignty, and how do they affect economic growth?
- How does "domestic dependent" status (trusteeship) affect economic development?
- What are the limits of state jurisdiction when Indians and non-Indians interact across tribal boundaries?

Tribal Sovereignty over Reservation Lands

Tribal sovereignty gives tribes the opportunity to craft their legal structures in ways that adhere to traditional tribal customs and culture while integrating tribal economies with outside trading partners. Steven Cornell and Joseph Kalt, members of the Harvard Project on American Indian Economic Development, conclude that "tribal constitutional forms appear to be keys to development. Development takes hold when the forms provide for the separations of power and when their structures match indigenous norms of political legitimacy."[4] If tribes have sovereign authority, they can choose governance structures that match their norms. However, if the governance structures are not stable or if they conflict with expectations of trading partners, sovereignty can thwart development.

Although tribes call themselves sovereign nations, they have limited jurisdiction over their lives and lands. Since *Cherokee Nation v. Georgia* in 1831, when tribes were designated "domestic dependent nations" and the relationship between individual Indians and the federal government was decreed to be "that of a ward to his guardian," Native Americans have been treated as if they are incompetent and incapable. Indeed, the Burke Act of 1906 that requires the government to assess whether Indians are "competent and capable" enough to be landowners remains part of federal Indian law today. *Johnson v. M'Intosh* (1823) affirmed that Europeans acquired ownership of the Americas through the "Doctrine of Discovery," and that doctrine was cited by the Supreme Court as recently as 2005, in *City of Sherrill v. Oneida Indian Nation of New York*, to undermine Indian land rights.[5]

Developing any and all trust resources in Indian Country requires approval by the Secretary of the Department of the Interior, a slow and costly procedure. The Southern Ute Tribe, for example, complains that its tribal oil company can typically begin oil production in three months when drilling off-reservation, but must wait three years for approval to drill on the reservation. Due to federal red tape, the tribe can more easily drill for oil ten thousand feet below the Gulf of Mexico than in its own backyard.[6]

In the *McGirt v. Oklahoma* case referenced above, the Supreme Court's minority, led by Chief Justice Roberts, reinforces the ward-guardian notion. Justice Roberts opined that recognizing land as a reservation complicates governance. This is true, but only because the Supreme Court and Congress continue to treat tribes as domestic dependent nations rather than full territorial sovereigns, free from external control and able to self-govern. The majority opinion in *McGirt* does confirm that tribes possess the sovereign power to establish their own governance structures and their own investment environments, but wardship is the antithesis of sovereignty. The two cannot mutually coexist, and in practice throughout Indian Country, wardship dominates.

Trusteeship and Economic Development

The deterrent effect of trusteeship on investment and development cannot be overstated. Most Indian land in the United States—approximately fifty-six million acres—is, or at some point was, reservation land set apart by treaty or statute for the use and benefit of tribal nations. In terms of property rights, beneficial interest in the lands belongs to tribes or individuals, but legal title belongs to the United States (see chapter 3). Only the federal government can sell, transfer, or in any way encumber the land for use by non-Indians. The United States is also responsible for the administration, control, and management of Indian lands and resources, functions it performs through the BIA in the US Department of the Interior. In most cases, although tribal governments play a role in land-management decisions, BIA officials have the final say on proposed uses by non-Indians, including permits or leases, charges to third parties, and financing agreements.

The BIA's Division of Land Titles and Records (DLTR) is responsible for over ten million acres belonging to individual Indians and forty-six million acres held in trust or restricted status for tribes. In 2015, the DLTR reported that sixty-one thousand land and resource management transaction approvals and recordings are conducted by the BIA each year.[7] The sheer magnitude of oversight and administration makes it significantly more difficult and time-consuming to obtain records, to negotiate land-use agreements, to generate interest in Indian lands, to transfer interests, and to finance investment.

In 2000, an amendment to the Indian Tribal Economic Development and Contract Encouragement Act (25 U.S.C.A. § 81) eliminated the requirement of approval by the Secretary of the Interior for contracts that encumber Indian land for seven years or less. While certainly an improvement, the amendment does not apply to large-scale, long-term endeavors like development of energy, mineral, or agricultural resources. For most projects, it is still the case that the BIA must be involved in all stages of land-related agreements, and very little can be done with tribal lands without the agency's direct, ongoing, and time-consuming involvement and approval.

The BIA, through its DLTR, is also the registry of Indian lands, and the recorder of transactions and rights and interests in those lands. Investors in Indian Country are often wary of the DLTR, uncertain about its approach to determining priority for interests, its efficiency in delivering registrations, and its ability to provide the level of legal certainty and confidence that is provided in most state titling systems.

Gaps in the Legal Framework on Tribal Land

Gaps in reservations' legal frameworks create uncertainty that discourages investment and economic development. Table 4.1 identifies common legal gaps that raise costs for investors

TABLE 4.1. Legal Framework for Investments

Investment Process	Legal Framework Requirements	Possible Gaps in Legal Framework	
		Off Tribal Land	On Tribal Land
Setting the terms of the deal	• Governance (who to work with). • Property right acquisition costs (rental, lease, fee simple). • Property right terms and conditions (rental, lease, fee simple). • Taxes, fees, and charges (property taxes, business taxes, service taxes, fees, and charges).	Processes, costs, timelines, and applicable taxes, fees, and charges, are clear.	Processes for development and costs of obtaining approvals and acquiring property rights, including tax and fee information and timelines, are often missing.
Government planning and approvals	• Land-use laws. • Development-approval processes. • Development-servicing standards. • Environmental requirements. • Heritage management and protection.	Land-use bylaws, clear laws, and processes for development applications, subdivision approvals, servicing requirements, and environmental and heritage requirements are the norm.	Laws and processes often missing or weak.
Government services and infrastructure	• Local services laws. • Financial management laws. • Core service requirements, including fire, water, and sewer. • Infrastructure financing.	Laws are routine and services are in place.	Significant variation among reservations. Only a few have a complete legal framework.
Financing and construction	• Mortgaging and financing requirements for rentals, leases, and sales. • Building codes and permits. • Builder's lien rights.	Clear local and state legal framework.	Financing and construction legal framework is piecemeal on most lands. Unclear application of state laws often creates additional uncertainty.

Source: Adapted from Tulo Centre of Indigenous Economics, *Building a Competitive First Nation Investment Climate* (Kamloops, BC: Tulo Centre of Indigenous Economics, 2014), 113, https://www.tulo.ca.

considering land-development projects. The table includes the law and contract requirements for a typical development deal as it progresses through the planning, approvals, financing, and construction stages.

Components of Investment-Supporting Legal Frameworks

Business transactions in the United States rest on confidence in state legal frameworks. Investment-friendly frameworks consist of three broad categories of state and local law: laws that support private property rights, laws that provide public regulation of property rights, and laws that support public services. Within these broad categories are regulations ranging from land-use and development constraints to resource use and environmental protection requirements.

Tribal sovereignty exempts reservations from state jurisdiction, leaving tribal governments to create their own frameworks—a task that many tribes have done poorly, and some not at all. Table 4.2 provides an overview of the types of state laws and services that encourage investment and note the gaps that occur because of tribal exemption from state law.

The federal government, with its exclusive jurisdiction over Indian lands, could legislate to fill all the gaps in tribal frameworks, but there is no requirement that it do so. Such action, in addition to being inconsistent with the current policy of self-determination, is hardly encouraged by the poor historical record of federal oversight and administration. Although Congress has addressed some of the areas through enacting direct legislation, such as federal building and fire codes, or by enabling tribal governments to make tribal law in specified areas, there remain extensive gaps in key areas of land use, property governance, and service provision. Regardless of the reasons for the gaps, tribes must learn to fill them if they want to facilitate investment.

TABLE 4.2. Property Laws and State Services Necessary for Economic Development

	Property Laws	
State Legislative Area	*Description*	*Application*
Real property law	Laws that create rules of the game or modify common-law principles provide the foundation for real property dealings. Included in this category are laws respecting how land and interests in land are owned, transferred, pledged, subdivided, leased, and foreclosed, as well as rules for transfers, charges, mortgages, and easements.	The rules of the game that prevail in the surrounding states are not applicable on reservations. While a number of tribal governments have successfully adopted compatible legal frameworks or are in the process of doing so, the vast majority have not.
Registration, survey, and subdivision of land	Laws that establish the land-title system and govern all aspects of land transactions, including rules respecting land surveys and strata subdivision, and transfer procedures, forms, requirements, and assurances.	These laws do not apply on tribal lands. Land surveys and deed registries are maintained by the BIA.
Civil law	A broad group of state and local laws regulate civil matters off-reservation. These include laws respecting personal property security interests, court order enforcement, family matters and child custody, and employment standards.	In most cases, existing federal legislation applies state and civil legislation does not apply on reservations unless specific agreements exist with tribal governments (like those found in state-tribal gaming contracts).
Wills, estates, and trusts	Laws establishing rules and procedures for making wills, estate administration, creating and settling trusts, and the duties of trusteeship.	Some aspects of these laws could apply on some tribal lands. In some areas, such as wills and estates of Indians residing on tribal lands, existing federal legislation applies.
Expropriation	Laws that set out the processes for expropriation and identify the specific expropriation powers of governments and other entities.	These laws do not apply on reservations. Federal laws govern expropriation on tribal land. Of additional concern to investors is that tribal courts may have jurisdiction in property disputes.
Natural resource regulation	Laws that govern the exploration, development, and exploitation of natural resources including water, mines, minerals, forestry, and oil and gas.	Specific federal legislation covers natural resource regulation on reservations. State laws that add constraints beyond those of federal legislation do not apply on tribal lands.

Property Laws

State Legislative Area	Description	Application
Land-use regulation and development control	State laws create an extensive regulatory framework that is often enhanced by delegated local government regulation. Regulation typically covers planning, zoning, building size and siting, development, sign regulation, tree-cutting regulation, and subdivision servicing and control.	These laws do not apply on tribal lands. Few tribal governments have comprehensive legislation in these areas.
Environmental management and assessment	Laws setting requirements for environmental management and protection (including investigations, completion of profiles, and remediation of contaminated sites) and environmental assessments for projects.	Federal environmental legislation applies on tribal lands, but state regulations do not.
Heritage conservation	Laws setting out rules and procedures for identification, designation, and conservation of heritage sites and artifacts.	Federal cultural and heritage legislation applies on tribal lands, but state regulations do not.

State Services

State Services and Regulation	Description	Application
Building codes	Laws applying building codes, providing systems of issuing building permits and inspection, and providing for the registration of builders' liens.	These laws do not apply on reservations. Some tribal governments have adopted their own regulations, but these may or may not differ from those of the state in which the reservation is located.
Fire regulation and safety standards	Laws creating the fire code, appointing fire personnel, and establishing fire safety requirements and inspections. Laws setting standards for electrical, gas, boilers, refrigeration, pressure valves and pipes, amusement rides, etc. and persons doing regulated work.	These laws do not apply on reservations. Some tribal governments have adopted their own regulations, but these may or may not differ from those of the state in which the reservation is located. Other reservations depend on BIA administration.

continued

Table 4.2 (*continued*)

State Services		
State Services and Regulation	*Description*	*Application*
Local services	Services including water, sewer, drainage, and waste management are typically provided by local governments within state constraints.	Most tribal governments are unable to provide the local services investors expect off-reservation. For many tribes, "local" services are the purview of the BIA.
Health and safety	Laws to ensure the health, safety and the protection of persons and property and to regulate the use of public places.	State and local laws do not apply on tribal lands. The majority of tribal governments do not fill this gap and default to BIA administration of federal policy.
Land taxation and assessment	Laws setting out the powers and framework for real property assessment and taxation of land. These taxes raise revenues for local services, schools, and health services.	State laws do not apply on reservation lands. Although they have the power to tax, most tribes do not have the population or level of development for a tax base to effectively support these services and therefore rely on BIA provision.

Source: Tulo Centre of Indigenous Economics, *Building a Competitive First Nation Investment Climate,* (Kamloops, BC: Tulo Centre of Indigenous Economics, 2014), 120–22, https://www.tulo.ca. Adjusted by the authors to reflect US conditions.

Sovereign Immunity Affects Economic Development

Indian tribes in the United States are immune from suit by virtue of their federally recognized status as sovereign entities. In the 1998 decision in *Kiowa Tribe v. Manufacturing Techs Inc.*, the Supreme Court extended this immunity to encompass not just governmental activities but also tribes' commercial activities, whether on or off the reservation. In a 5–4 decision in the 2014 case of *Michigan v. Bay Mills Indian Community*, the Court affirmed *Kiowa* on the grounds that Congress has the sole power to impose limitations on tribal sovereignty but has consistently chosen not to do so.

Although sovereign immunity is fundamental to preserving tribes' identity and independence, it can be nonetheless problematic from the perspective of economic development. In his dissent to *Kiowa*, Justice Stevens decried the Kiowas' use of tribal sovereignty as a means to escape liability when they defaulted on a promissory note. Stevens prophetically commented that the majority decision upholding the sovereignty defense raised a red flag to investors and entrepreneurs considering whether to do business with tribes and tribal corporations.[8]

The 2011 case of *Seneca Telephone Company v. Miami Tribe* arose when the Seneca Telephone Company's underground telephone lines on the Miami reservation were damaged by the tribe's excavation project. As in *Kiowa*, there was no dispute that the tribe had caused the damage, and again, as in *Kiowa*, the Seneca Company's suit to recover damages and attorneys' fees was dismissed when the Miami tribe asserted tribal sovereignty. The Court recognized the injustice of the company's having no recourse despite the appropriateness of their claims of negligence against the tribe, but again it professed to be bound by the lack of congressional direction. Expressing the same frustrations evident in the *Kiowa* and *Bay Mills* decisions, the Court's *Seneca* decision pointedly called on Congress to pass legislation limiting tribal immunity in cases of clear negligence.

In the absence of congressional definition, tribes continue to probe the limits of sovereign immunity, and the courts continue to wrestle with the issue. In 2017, the federal courts struck down a Mohawk tribe's use of sovereign immunity to generate income by shielding a nontribal enterprise. Allergan, maker of Restasis eye drops, transferred ownership of six patents to the St. Regis Mohawk Tribe. The tribe received a $17.5 million origination fee with the understanding that Allergan would retain the exclusive right to lease back the patents for $15 million annually. Generic drug companies objected to this as an attempt to use sovereign immunity to avoid the Hatch-Waxman Act's timeline for ending exclusivity and allowing generic manufacture. Mylan Pharmaceuticals took the case to the US Patent and Trademark Office and then to the US Federal Circuit Court of Appeals, both of which rejected the tribe's motion to terminate the proceedings on the basis of sovereign immunity. In April 2019, the Supreme Court denied the Mohawks' petition for review, thus upholding the lower court's decisions.[9]

Ironically, while Congress has yet to clarify the reach of sovereign immunity, many tribes have improved their investment climates by voluntarily waiving it. Typically, waivers are limited in scope and negotiated on a project-by-project basis. It is now quite common for nontribal entities to require at least a limited waiver before contracting with a tribe. Tribal corporations and other entities created under tribal law may also waive immunity, and the courts have ruled that they may do so without affecting the overall immunity of the tribe.

Limited waivers of sovereign immunity typically specify who is entitled to bring a claim, the types of claims allowed, the types and amounts of damages allowed, the law to be applied in hearing claims, and the forum in which claims may be heard. Tribes tend to prefer that tribal law govern contracts and that disputes be heard in tribal courts. Nontribal contractors often prefer state law, arguing that tribal law is less developed. They also complain that there is no up-to-date repository of tribal law, making it much harder to research, increasing uncertainty, and raising the cost of settling disputes.

If agreement cannot be reached about the applicable law and dispute forum, there is also the option of binding or nonbinding arbitration. Tribes may be reluctant to agree to arbitration, however, as there is uncertainty over whether such agreements imply a waiver of immunity. The Supreme Court in 2001's *C & L Enterprises, Inc. v. Citizen Band Potawatomi Indian Tribe of Oklahoma* held that the tribe waived its sovereign immunity by entering into a contract that clearly specified dispute arbitration. The ruling established the requirement of clarity, identifying three essential elements to uphold contracts incorporating dispute arbitration: "an agreement to arbitrate all disputes, an agreement to be bound by any arbitration award, and an agreement that any award could be enforced in any state or federal court with jurisdiction."[10]

Of further concern to potential investors is that tribes may or may not have developed commercial codes, that such codes may contain inconsistencies with tribal law, and that tribal courts may not function as independent, nonpolitical bodies. Outside Indian Country, secured transactions fall within state jurisdiction and are covered by Article 9 of the Universal Commercial Code (UCC), which has been adopted by all fifty states. While not exact copies, the state commercial codes are substantially uniform. That uniformity reduces risk by reducing creditors' uncertainty and the costs of commercial agreements. Congress has not specified a commercial code for Indian nations, so it is up to each tribe to create its own. The result is a hodgepodge. Some tribes have no secured-transactions laws; some have comprehensive codes with features unique to the tribal culture; some have no comprehensive code but do have components such as rules covering repossession. Furthermore, some tribes have adopted the official text of Article 9 of the UCC, and some have adopted the version of the UCC used in the state in which the tribe resides.

Recognizing that the lack of a uniform code may discourage investment, the Uniform Law Commission's Committee on Liaison with American Indian Tribes and Nations assembled in 2001 a drafting committee comprised of commissioners, representatives from ten tribes, and other advisors with experience in tribal legal and development issues and tasked them with creating a secured-transactions template that tribes might adopt without bearing the expense of drafting their own. The result, the Model Tribal Secured Transactions Act, or MTSTA (completed in August 2005 and revised in 2017), is largely based on Article 9 of the UCC but addresses unique tribal issues such as exemption of sacred items from covered property; coordination with other tribal laws; incorporation of tribal customs and traditions, like the tribal "business day," for example; and acknowledgment of tribal sovereign immunity.[11]

Tribal sovereign immunity may also deprive tribes and their partner investors of bankruptcy protection, increasing the risks of investment and the costs of business failure. The question of whether tribes themselves can declare bankruptcy has been settled, for now, by a precedent established in a 2012 federal court decision against the Santa Ysabel Diegueño Indians. They filed for Chapter 11 bankruptcy protection after their small casino had to pay out a $1,036,253 jackpot in 2011. The Southern District of California bankruptcy court ruled the tribe ineligible for protection under US bankruptcy law because it fit none of the eligible categories defined in the code (US Code, Title 11).

The question of whether bankruptcy protection is available to tribal corporations, however, remains unsettled. Sa'Nyu Wa, the economic development corporation of the Hualapai Tribe that owns the Grand Canyon Skywalk, was successfully sued by the developer for $28 million in ticket sales owed under the 2003 development contract, and in 2013 a federal judge upheld the judgment. On appeal, Sa'Nyu Wa argued that it was a corporation, not a government, and therefore eligible to file for Chapter 11. The case was eventually settled without the court commenting on the bankruptcy eligibility of tribal corporations, so the uncertainty about bankruptcy protection for tribal enterprises persists.

Jurisdictional Issues Affecting Economic Development

Contemporary federal, state, local, and tribal governments' jurisdiction over Indian affairs continues to be based on judicial interpretation of the Constitution's provisions and is plagued by change, confusion, and conflict. In the modern era of Indian self-determination, one ongoing issue concerns tribal enterprises located within reservation boundaries that market products to non-Indian customers who would be subject to state taxation and regulation if they purchased the same products off-reservation.

In 1980, the Supreme Court ruled in *Washington v. Confederated Tribes of the Colville Indian Reservation* that the state of Washington was allowed to impose retail sales taxes on reservation-located cigarette sales to non-Indians, that the tribal smoke shops were required to collect them for the state, and that the state was within its powers when it seized cigarette shipments to the reservation after the Colvilles refused to collect the tax. The court's reasoning directly addressed the key issues of trusteeship, self-governance, and preemption:

> The Tribes' involvement in the operation and taxation of cigarette marketing on the reservation does not oust the State from any power to exact its sales and cigarette taxes from nonmembers purchasing cigarettes at tribal smokeshops. Principles of federal Indian law, whether stated in terms of pre-emption, tribal self-government, or otherwise, do not authorize Indian tribes to market an exemption from state taxation to persons who would normally do their business elsewhere. . . . Washington does not infringe the right of reservation Indians to make their own laws and be ruled by them, merely because the result of imposing taxes will be to deprive the Tribes of revenues which they currently are receiving. . . . Although the result of these taxes will be to lessen or eliminate tribal commerce with nonmembers, that market existed in the first place only because of a claimed exemption for these very taxes. Such taxes do not burden commerce that would exist on the reservations without respect to the tax exemption.[12]

Unfortunately, the Court's decision addressed only the specific case and provided no clear guideline as to when tribal economic endeavors involving non-Indians were and were not subject to state law. Thus the issue was bound to arise again. In the same year as the Colville decision, the Ninth US Circuit Court of Appeals heard a combined case brought by the White Mountain Apache against the state of Arizona and by the Colville tribes against the state of Washington in which both claimed the right to preempt state governments' power to require that non-Indians hunting and fishing on a reservation with the Indians' permission must purchase state licenses and abide by state game and fish regulations. The tribes argued that their economic development was being undermined as both tribal and private revenue were reduced by the states' actions.

The Apache and Colville tribes market the opportunity for non-Indian sportsmen to hunt and fish on their large reservations in Arizona and Washington, respectively. The tribes sell these sportsmen tribal hunting and fishing licenses, and they also profit from sales of food, lodging, and services. Both tribes have detailed hunting and fishing codes, which purport to make state law inapplicable to non-Indian sportsmen on the reservation.[13]

Arizona and Washington acknowledged that the tribes are sovereign over Indian people within the reservation boundaries and that tribal governments could, if they wished, prohibit non-Indians from hunting or fishing on the reservations, or require them to purchase licenses and abide by tribal regulations. However, the states argued that requiring non-Indians to purchase state licenses was a violation neither of tribal sovereignty nor of the federal government's policy of encouraging tribal self-sufficiency and economic development.

In 1981, the Supreme Court sided with the White Mountain Apache and the Confederated Colville tribes against the states, but again refrained from identifying guidelines as to when state actions that affect tribal revenue violate the Constitution's Commerce Clause. The Court directed, instead, that such cases "are to be settled . . . by weighing in the judicial scales the present-day state, federal, and tribal interests involved."[14] Requiring a case-by-case examination did little to reduce investors' uncertainty over the cost of doing business in Indian country.

Complicating the cigarette sales, wildlife licensing, and similar commerce cases is Public Law 280 and its subsequent amendments. The original 1953 legislation removed federal jurisdiction over reservations in six states and mandated that those states' governments assume civil and criminal jurisdiction over the reservations within their boundaries. Later the option was given to all states, along with the choice of assuming either complete or partial jurisdiction—and ten assumed some degree of jurisdiction, further complicating the judicial picture.[15] Washington's P.L. 280 decision to assume only criminal jurisdiction played a role in the Colville licensing cases, and California's status as a P.L. 280 mandatory state played a role in judicial conflict over state and tribal jurisdiction in perhaps the most well-known of Indian economic endeavors—casino gambling.

Jurisdictional Conflict Case Study: Gaming

The phenomenon of Indian gaming started in 1975 with the Oneida Indian Nation's decision to fund their fire department with bingo games, a practice common among New York nonprofits. Bingo operations spread to other tribes in other states. Tribal operations started competing with nontribal games by offering larger prizes than allowed by state law, claiming that tribal sovereignty exempted them from state gambling regulations. *California v. Cabazon Band of Mission Indians* was the first such case to reach the Supreme Court, which ruled in 1987 that California could not ban or regulate Indian gaming unless congressional legislation explicitly authorized the state to do so. To California's argument that as a mandatory Public Law 280 state it had both criminal and civil jurisdiction over Indian lands, the Court responded that

extending that state's laws over the gaming operations of the Cabazon and Morongo Bands of Mission Indians would amount to an exercise of

power that was civil and regulatory, rather than criminal and prohibi-
tory. As such, California's bingo laws were not applicable to the gaming
operations on Indian lands in California. . . . Although California had
an interest in preventing unscrupulous persons from participating in
gambling, the federal and tribal interests in tribal self-determination
and economic self-sufficiency were stronger . . . [and] the state's interests had to give way.[16]

The explosion of Indian gaming—over a hundred operations
with annual revenues in excess of $100 million by the mid-1980s—
brought pressure on Congress from states that relied on gaming
revenue, saw unrestricted Indian gambling as competition, and
feared that crime and corruption would accompany the building and operation of casinos. In 1988, using the Constitution's
Commerce Clause power, Congress passed the IGRA, the Indian
Gaming Regulatory Act, clarifying that states could not deprive
Indian tribes of their right to offer and regulate gaming on their
own lands if the games were not specifically prohibited by federal
law and if gambling—of any type—was legal within the state.

The act also created the National Indian Gaming Commission
to regulate tribal casinos, prevent the entry of organized crime,
and ensure that the tribes are the economic beneficiaries of tribal
gaming. It also authorized Indian casinos to offer Las Vegas–style
games and slot machines. However, in a blow to tribal sovereignty,
the legislation requires that tribes request and negotiate a tribal-
state compact outlining the terms of gaming. Thirty-one states currently have such compacts.[17] While the law mandates that the states
negotiate in good faith, disputes are common and thus another
source of increasing costs of investment.

Foxwoods, reputed to be the world's largest and most profitable
casino, exemplifies how the IGRA restricted tribal sovereignty but
also opened the way for tribal enterprises with the potential to generate huge returns on investment.

In 1989, the Pequot Tribe requested a gambling compact with the state of Connecticut, which refused to negotiate until ordered to do so by the US Court of Appeals. In the ensuing negotiations, the Pequots acknowledged the state's interest in preventing an increase in casino-related crimes. They agreed to let Connecticut have authority over alcohol and drug use on casino grounds, to allow state police patrols and crime-control operations, and to require that casino employees be licensed by the Connecticut Department of Special Revenue. In return, the state agreed that the Pequots would retain all control over the business operations, the size of the casino, the number of tables, and the hours of operation. Connecticut agreed that the Pequots would not pay state taxes, allowing them to keep all remaining profits after reimbursing the state for the regulatory activities. Unfortunately, the agreement foundered on Connecticut's insistence that the state prohibition of slot machines extend to the reservation. Secretary of the Interior Manuel Lujan Jr. countered Connecticut's refusal to sign the compact by declaring the federal government's regulatory prerogative to allow a casino on the Pequot Reservation, exempt from state taxation. The Supreme Court refused to hear the state's appeal.

The casino was an immediate success.

Ten months . . . [after opening in February 1992], the casino had not yet spent a single hour closed; customers were gambling twenty-four hours a day. Each day approximately thirteen thousand people flocked to Foxwoods . . . [which] was often so crowded that patrons had to wait hours for a seat at the gaming tables. . . . The casino had ballooned to thirty-five hundred employees, constituting a $60 million payroll. In its first year in operation, the booming casino was on its way to generating significantly more than the $100 million in gross revenue that had been projected. Demand was so great that in July of 1992, only five months after Foxwoods opened, the Pequots embarked on a $142 million expansion of the complex.[18]

Facing an economic downturn, a huge budget shortfall, and pressure from non-Indian bingo establishments—whose owners pointed out that Connecticut was losing taxes not only on casino profits but also on casino employees' personal income—the state legalized casino gambling in 1993. Facing the possibility of competition from Las Vegas and Atlantic City casino investors, the Pequots negotiated an agreement to pay the state, annually, the greater of 25 percent of slot-machine revenue or $100 million in return for the exclusive right to slot-machine gambling in the state. Foxwoods installed slot machines, and its revenue surged to near $1 billion in its second full year of operation.

While the Foxwoods story is ultimately one of triumph for the tribe, it is also a cautionary tale of the jurisdictional conflict and uncertainty that dog tribal efforts to jump-start development in the face of state opposition. In another example, Florida refused to negotiate a gaming compact with the Seminole Tribe in 1991, and the tribe sued. Eventually the Supreme Court ruled that by allowing tribes to sue when states refused to negotiate a compact, the IGRA violated the Eleventh Amendment. The *Seminole Tribe v. Florida* decision meant that tribes could no longer force states to negotiate gaming compacts in good faith. States responded by demanding shares of gaming revenue. Subsequently, the Secretary of the Interior required that revenue-sharing compacts must grant tribes some level of exclusivity. This softened the blow from *Seminole*, but fewer states were willing to enter compact negotiations, and those that did took a very hard line in demanding revenue and jurisdictional concessions from the tribes.

In addition to jurisdictional conflicts that stifle investment, the gaming industry suffers from being outside the standard procedures and protections that can be accessed by off-reservation businesses. Foxwoods, for example, suffered from the economic recession of 2008, but could not use the bankruptcy and refinancing options available to off-reservation enterprises to manage its $2 billion debt to bondholders. Tribes are ineligible for bankruptcy restructuring because they are not included as a class of debtors in the US Bankruptcy Code. Because of tribal sovereignty, and because nontribal ownership of casinos is prohibited by IGRA, struggling casinos also cannot sell off tribal trust assets to raise capital or swap their debt for equity. Their only option is the difficult process of restructuring the debt by negotiating directly with their creditors.[19]

Economic Leakage

A well-functioning, growing economy exhibits virtuous cycles of self-reinforcing positive events. Successful investment generates employment and income, which generate consumer spending, which in turn generates more investment. Unfortunately, the majority of tribal economies miss out on the multiplier effect of virtuous cycles because the benefits of consumer spending leak off the reservation to bordering communities.

As Gavin Clarkson of New Mexico State University explains, off-reservation communities, not tribal economies, are the most common beneficiaries of Indian spending. When $1 million is invested in most communities, it generates approximately $10 million of cash flow. In Indian Country, however, a $1 million investment typically generates just $1 million of cash flow. The largest Walmart on the planet, in terms of dollar sales per square foot, is in Gallup, New Mexico, on the edge of the Navajo Nation.[20] Gallup is a town of fewer than twenty-five thousand. Its Walmart's customer base, however, is closer to seventy-five thousand, a number swollen by the lack of shopping alternatives for nearby reservation residents.

> Social Security checks are distributed to the elders and veterans on [the first of the month] . . . and most tribal members have neither access to a local bank nor sufficient consumer-spending options on the reservation. Most Navajos therefore end up driving for an hour or more to

purchase much needed groceries, lumber, auto parts, and children's school clothes in border towns such as Gallup. According to a 2006 study conducted by the University of New Mexico Bureau of Business and Economic Analysis, significant competition for retail dollars from the Navajo Nation is spread among several surrounding non-Indian communities, including Gallup, Grants, Farmington, Show Low, and Winslow.[21]

Recent surveys by the Diné Policy Institute found that 60 percent of the components of the Navajo daily diet are not available on the reservation, so 80 percent of residents purchased groceries in off-reservation towns, for some a three-hundred-mile round trip. Overall, 71 percent of Navajo dollars are spent off-reservation. For the neighboring Zuni Pueblo, the figure is 84 percent.[22]

Leakage is the rule rather than the exception for tribal economies. Income from government benefits, tribal enterprises, and tribal resources is spent in border communities. In the case of many larger tribes, the losses to the tribe and the benefits to the surrounding communities and the state are far from trivial. The second-largest Walmart is in Billings, Montana, near the Crow reservation. "The former chairman of the Crow Nation in Montana suggested to the *Billings Gazette* that 'if anyone doubts that money flows into Billings [from the Crow Nation], go to Wal-Mart today after members receive their per-capita check from the tribe. We don't call it Wal-Mart, we call it 'Crow-Mart.'"[23] A 2001 study by Montana tribes found that tribal and BIA incomes leak more than $200 million annually, generating between $3 and $5 billion for the state's economy.[24]

Credit Deserts on Reservations

Trust status means both that land cannot be used as collateral to fund tribal endeavors and that individuals cannot use home equity to secure entrepreneurial ventures. The reluctance of banks and other financial institutions to make capital available without property-based collateral renders most reservations credit deserts. Without access to traditional financing, tribes and individuals struggle to find start-up and expansion capital to stop leakage.

A 2019 report by the US Department of the Interior's Assistant Secretary for Indian Affairs acknowledges that "affordable credit is a daunting problem in Indian Country. Eighty-six percent of tribal lands do not have a bank and 15 percent of American Indian and Alaska Natives live 100 miles or more from one. Of financial institutions on or near tribal communities, only 33 percent offer start-up loans, only 29 percent offer small business loans, and just 26 percent offer micro business loans."[25] The most recent figures available, from 2013, indicate that more than 50 percent of nonreservation adults bank online. Few reservation residents can bridge the digital divide; the Federal Communications Commission estimates that less than 10 percent of reservations have broadband access.[26] Unable to pry open the door to financing, tribes and individuals struggle to find start-up and expansion capital to offer on-reservation alternatives to Indian consumers.[27]

While tribal economies would seem a huge untapped market, banks have been reluctant to breach the "buckskin curtain," preferring instead to locate in border towns. The 2001 Report of the Native American Lending Study was the first to document on a national level the limited or nonexistent access to capital and credit in Indigenous communities on the mainland and in Alaska and Hawaii. The report, by the Treasury Department's Community Development Financial Institutions Fund, identifies a number of cultural barriers that, in addition to the problem of trust status, arise from and contribute to Indians' separation from the off-reservation financial world. Common barriers include inflexible bank rules and regulations that are incompatible with Indigenous cultural practices and/or the income patterns of reservation communities; Native Americans' limited experience with finance and lack of sound credit histories; lenders' and investors' unfamiliarity with tribal governance, courts, and bureaucracies; historical lack of trust between tribes and banks; and discrimination against and stereotyping of Native Americans.

On those reservations where economic conditions are improving, banks are showing more interest in this untapped market. Also encouraging is the number of tribes moving to own or control their own banks rather than waiting for traditional institutions to catch up to Native communities' needs. The nonprofit-owned Indian Land Capital Company (ILCC), for example, is compiling a record of success in funding tribal projects through agreements compatible with tribal communities' practices and seasonally variable income patterns. The ILCC has also found ways around the problems of trust status and tribal sovereignty. "Unlike traditional lending institutions, ILCC lends to tribes based on 'full faith and credit.' As such, ILCC does not require land to be used as collateral for the loan but rather encumbers alternative streams of income, including business or land revenue."[28]

For-profit Indian institutions are also finding creative ways to collateralize loans and secure transactions. The majority owner of Borrego Springs Bank, N.A., is the Viejas Band of Kumeyaay Indians, whose 3,500 members occupy a 1,600-acre reservation east of San Diego. Like the ILCC, Borrego Springs Bank finds ways to lend without encumbering land and without exposing itself to unacceptable levels of risk.

> In one case, the tribe purchased several certificates of deposit (CDs), which the bank uses as collateral for loans to individual tribal members. . . . Loan applications for this program are reviewed by a three-person tribal committee for traditional lending criteria, like repayment ability. Tribal loan applicants also are expected to put up whatever assets they might own for collateral, like a car. Such assets do

not necessarily have to equal the value of the loan . . . but the intent is to create some accountability for the loan recipient.[29]

Some bankers have successfully negotiated leases with tribal entities and taken leasehold mortgage interests as collateral. Bankers also have worked around the issue of securing loans on trust lands by using collateralized deposits from sources such as tribal reserve funds and certificates of deposit. When tribes with limited resources are not able to pledge reserve funds, some bankers instead use as collateral the equipment of the commercial enterprise for which the loan is made. Other examples of income streams that tribes have used to secure loans include third-party health care reimbursements, gaming revenue, income from extracting resources on the reservation, per capita payments, and presold goods and services.

Commercial Codes and Secured Transactions

Rules governing secured transactions are the purview of the states, and recognizing the benefits of uniformity, all fifty states have adopted similar versions of the United States' UCC, or Uniform Commercial Code. As tribal nations are not subject to state legislation, it is up to individual tribal governments to create commercial law and regulations. Progress in doing so is slow, or in some tribes nonexistent, greatly increasing lender uncertainty about the enforceability of collateralized contacts. Additionally, while some tribes have commercial codes and secured transactions laws, there is little uniformity and consistency across reservations. A 2016 report of the Office of the Comptroller of Currency cited "inconsistencies among tribal laws and regulations regarding secured transactions, resulting from a lack of formalized commercial practices and standardized documentation to be a major source of lender uncertainty."[30]

To address this deficiency, the MTSTA, or Model Tribal Secured Transactions Act, was developed in 2005 from Article 9 of the UCC as a template for tribes wishing to adopt secured transactions law that would be familiar to investors and less costly than developing their own. The purpose of the MTSTA is to address issues unique to tribes and reservations in a manner consistent with the practices already familiar to lenders and investors.

Standards such as those in the MTSTA increase business efficiency and confer significant investment and development benefits. They reduce uncertainty and transaction costs by boosting consumer confidence in particular products, services, and processes. That confidence then reduces costs associated with searching for information, assessing quality, and developing contracts or relationships. A common example is the use of standardized currency. We trust the value of our currency and this confidence reduces our costs because we do not need to assess its value before we use it. These benefits are among the reasons that countries seek standards in trade agreements and try to harmonize their systems. The benefits are so significant that almost all countries in the world are willing to accept common standards and forgo some of their sovereignty in exchange for the resulting increase in trade.

Standards can also create network interconnections. As the number of users of a standard increases, so does the number of associated innovations. A good example is the explosion of iPhone applications. As there are more users of iPhones, there is greater incentive for developers to create applications. Additionally, standards can reduce the costs of production. Established standards allow users to learn by doing and become more proficient as they specialize in a task or process, creating economies of scale and reducing production costs.

Investors benefit from standards because they support harmonization with adjacent jurisdictions. When standards achieve national or regional harmonization, investors' research and legal costs fall. The benefit to tribes of adopting financial management standards is the increased investor confidence in tribal fiscal systems and reduced perception of risk.

Building an Investment-Friendly Economy

Most tribes in the United States have relatively small populations— the vast majority number under five thousand, and some have fewer than one hundred—with insufficient resources to build their own comprehensive legal frameworks from the ground up and insufficient administrative capacity to exercise the full scope of their regulatory powers. Models like the MTSTA help tribes fill gaps in their legal frameworks. As tribes seek to improve their investment climates by developing or refining their legal frameworks, four objectives should guide their efforts.

- *Protecting jurisdiction.* Tribal governments should have the authority to create or implement their legal frameworks on their lands. This enables them to preserve jurisdiction over tribal lands, and to promote their comparative or competitive regional advantage.
- *Increasing administrative efficiency.* Regulatory frameworks should reduce transaction costs for investors, be administratively efficient and cost-effective, and minimize switching costs (the costs of moving from the old system to the new one). It is therefore advantageous for them to provide for standardization, encourage best practices, and harmonize with other jurisdictions.
- *Increasing market value.* Regulatory options should raise the market value of tribal lands by increasing user familiarity and improving property-rights certainty.
- *Strengthening access to capital and improving local services.* Regulatory options should improve financing opportunities

by providing greater certainty to investors. They should also provide a revenue stream to raise the quality of local services.

There is no single recipe for constructing an investment-friendly institutional climate. As noted earlier, connecting a modern framework with a tribe's cultural roots is important. The good news is that the roots of traditional tribal economies offer many options for tribes to make this connection.

5

FROM A GRANTS ECONOMY TO A REVENUE ECONOMY

Both on and off reservations, there is growing awareness that federal dollars cannot generate sustainable wealth for tribes and their citizens or free them from dependency. Specialization and trade can, but, as discussed in previous chapters, wealth-generating markets require an enabling institutional framework including strong ownership claims to property, sound governance structures, and clear jurisdiction. All of these existed before European contact, but most are today weak or missing throughout Indian Country. Making reservation economies sustainable is also problematic because the fiscal and financial institutions that support investment and create private and public capital are missing.

Strong self-determination policies have two components. First, tribes must have secure and stable revenue streams in order to provide quality public services and infrastructure that support commerce. Investors looking for business opportunities off-reservation look to local and state governments for public infrastructure. They expect the same support from tribes, but for the most part, reservation governments do not have the dependable revenue streams necessary for infrastructure creation and maintenance.

Second, self-determination requires that citizens and businesses have access to capital. Banks and other lending institutions require collateral to secure loans, meaning that title to property must be transferable and judicial arbitration fair and impartial. Those requirements are generally unmet in Indian Country, where property rights are clouded by federal trusteeship and tribal courts are generally not firmly grounded in the rule of law.

The treaties that moved tribes onto reservations gave tribal governments neither fiscal power nor the ability to shape their economies. The door to autonomy remained firmly closed until the initiation of self-determination policies in the 1970s. Since then, some tribal governments, with the encouragement of the BIA, have taken steps to reclaim responsibility for collecting revenues and delivering services to their citizens. Some have seized the opportunity to develop their own revenue streams and provide public services and have made impressive progress. Others have taken tentative steps toward autonomy, but most tribes remain dependent, lacking the fiscal tools to shape their economies.

Tribal Fiscal Relationship to Federal and State Governments

Unfortunately, tribes' ongoing relationships with local, state, and federal governments make assertion of fiscal independence difficult and costly. Weak public-sector fiscal institutions in tribal government together with often inaccessible private-sector financial institutions are strong disincentives to potential investors and business partners and daunting impediments to individual and tribal entrepreneurship.

A transparent fiscal framework in which information is readily accessible strengthens the investment climate, whereas weak fiscal institutions foster uncertainty and underinvestment. In order to confidently predict future levels of taxation and other business costs, investors expect tribal governments to ensure that local services and infrastructure can be financed and maintained. They want access to transparent and reliable government fiscal reporting and to data necessary for revenue and cost projections. Key questions for investors include these:

- Which revenues does tribal government have the power to collect, and which are actually collected?
- How secure and stable are tribal revenue sources?
- How are tax rates and fees determined?
- How are government finances reported and managed?
- How are service and financial responsibilities distributed among tribal, local, state, and federal governments?
- How are government finances reported and managed?

Fiscal federalism—the relationship among local, state, and federal governments—defines which governments are empowered to collect specific revenues and which are responsible for specific services and infrastructure. Outside reservations, income and payroll taxes provide most of the revenue for the federal government; income, sales, and property taxes provide most state revenues; and property taxes and transfers from state and federal entities are the main sources of local government revenues. Tribal government of domestic dependent nations has never been a component of fiscal federalism, nor was it incorporated into the fiscal framework as Indian policy evolved through the twentieth century.

Without a fiscal framework to generate revenue, it is impossible for tribes to provide the investment climate for sustaining economic growth. Tribal governments generally do not have their own tax- and resource-generated revenues. As a result, they are stymied in asserting their own interests, obstructed from increasing capacity, and handcuffed in terms of developing services that meet their nations' own unique needs. Tribal fiscal power is entangled in disputes between the federal and state governments over service responsibilities for tribal citizens and over appropriate payment for services. Almost all tribal governments are dependent on federal grants as their major revenue source. Federal funds come with strings attached: terms and conditions that restrict tribal governments' flexibility. Transfers are often short term and create cumbersome administrative and accountability burdens. Throughout Indian Country, transfer-based funding is insufficient to support services and infrastructure comparable to those found in the rest of the nation.

Tribal governments' inability to demonstrate reliable fiscal power leaves potential investors' questions unanswered and increases uncertainty in the investment climate.

- What are the sources of tribal government revenue, and how much is collected?
- What are the tribal government's current and projected expenditures?
- What are the cost drivers of the identified expenditures?
- How do tribal expenditure levels and service quality compare to those of nearby local and state governments?
- What are the tribal government's deficits and debts?

The answers to these questions are at best costly to obtain and commonly not available at all. Throughout Indian Country, data collection is deficient or nonexistent, responsibilities for revenues and expenditures are poorly defined, and few tribes use standardized statistics or reporting formats. Tribal governments that successfully compete against off-reservation investment opportunities are those that demonstrate their fiscal competence by providing ready, clear, and standardized data collection and reporting.

From the Vicious Circle to the Virtuous Circle

Historically, the fiscal relationship of Indian tribes to the US government—characterized by unstable, unpredictable federal transfers; unimplemented treaty rights; poor or untrustworthy services; little access to long-term funds for infrastructure; and small amounts of discretionary revenues—has generated a *vicious* circle of dependent poverty. Figure 5.1 illustrates that improving this fiscal relationship is necessary for tribes to establish *virtuous* circles of investment and economic growth.

The left side of the figure depicts the fiscal cycle of poverty for most tribes. Due to limited revenue, infrastructure and services are substandard, which creates a poor investment climate that limits income for citizens and, consequently, limits tribal government revenue. Low income and revenue perpetuate the need for transfers, generating a vicious circle of transfer dependency.

To escape the vicious cycle and start the virtuous circle of investment and growth illustrated on the right side of the graphic, tribes need predictable transfer funding, access to nontransfer revenue and financing, and competent fiscal administration.

In the virtuous circle of investment and economic growth, secure revenue streams allow tribal governments to provide better services and infrastructure, leading to higher levels of investment. Investment, in turn, raises employment levels and incomes for citizens and increases revenue for tribal governments. Completing the circle initiates another iteration of the process. When the self-replicating cycle is firmly established, the cost of doing business on reservations falls, tribes gain access to long-term capital, and tribal autonomy increases. Enabling legislative and administrative frameworks, continuity of transfer funding, and capacity for direct

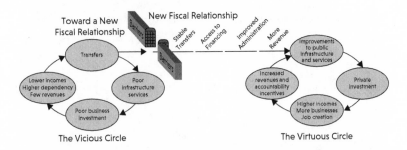

FIGURE 5.1. Toward a New Fiscal Relationship

Source: Tulo Centre of Indigenous Economics, *Building a Competitive First Nation Investment Climate* (Kamloops, BC: Tulo Centre of Indigenous Economics, 2014), 153, https://www.tulo.ca.

revenue generation are essential to tribes' efforts to initiate their own virtuous circles and escape dependency.

The sovereign decision making and fiscal power that are key to self-determination are also key to establishing a virtuous circle. Tribes experiencing success in engineering their own economic growth are those that have established control over their resources, development programs, and infrastructure. The Native Nations Institute summarizes what is necessary:

> While economic factors such as high educational attainment, access to markets, and natural resource endowments also can contribute to development, they tend to pay off after a Native nation has been able to bring decisions with local impact under local control and to structure capable, culturally legitimate institutions of self-government that can make and manage those decisions. The same can be said of federal grants, preferential treatment in the government procurement process, and tax or regulatory advantages (of which tribal gaming enterprises are one example). They are helpful inputs and policies, but they are not root causes of Native Community development; such opportunities yield lasting benefits when self-determined and self-governing Native nations are able to use them strategically.[1]

The extent to which tribal planning can successfully leverage assets, increase savings, and attract investment depends crucially on establishing fiscal power and improving access to credit and financial capital.

Infrastructure Investment Starts the Virtuous Circle

Public economic infrastructure, the physical capital and services provided by the public sector and paid for by public revenues, raises the return to private investment. Successful development, therefore, requires planning for dependable infrastructure—both ongoing local services like police and fire protection as well as construction and maintenance of physical infrastructure for clean water, waste collection and treatment, roads, and telecommunications. Such infrastructure improves the health of workers, reduces the costs of transportation and information, and raises the value of land by converting it from raw to serviced. Investments in water and sewer infrastructure, for example, lead to improved health and safety. Investments in transportation infrastructure can reduce congestion, travel costs, and time, meaning that workers can seek employment opportunities farther from home, which improves the matching of job requirements with the skills in the labor pool.

A 2016 report on taxation in Indian Country by the nonprofit Montana Budget and Policy Center identifies the public services tribal governments must provide to fully realize their sovereign quest for self-determination. Figure 5.2 captures the magnitude of the task.

While infrastructure construction is a Herculean task, tribes across the US are realizing significant returns to this type of public investment. A report by the National Congress of American Indians (NCAI) in 2017 highlighted "impressive stories of community revitalization and local and regional economic success empowered by strategic investments in infrastructure development."[2]

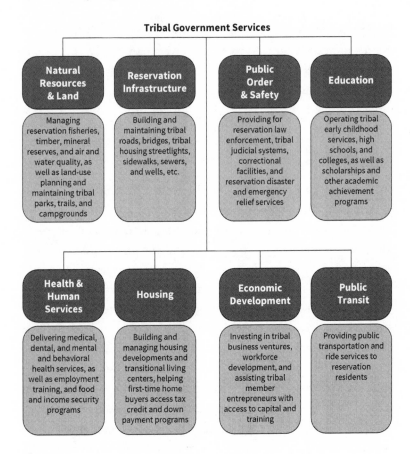

FIGURE 5.2. Tribal Government Services

For example, infrastructure investment created a path to economic well-being for the Mississippi Band of Choctaw Indians, whose poverty in the 1960s was even worse than what was typical throughout the rural South. Living conditions on the Band's reservation were deplorable—most houses were substandard, nine in ten had no indoor plumbing, and a third had no electricity. Seeking to uplift its community, the Band embarked on creating a diversified, sustainable economy, appropriately targeting provision of physical infrastructure as a critical first order of business. Fifty years later, the Band has not only transformed its reservation's quality of life, it has become a major economic engine in the region, employing thousands of Natives and non-Natives through its suite of Band-owned enterprises.[3]

Similarly, the Citizen Potawatomi Nation, located just east of Oklahoma City, profits greatly from commercial operations as a result of infrastructure investment. Forward-looking tribal leaders saw the importance of diversifying their economy and took the first steps by investing in both physical and intellectual infrastructure. Iron Horse Industrial Park was built on four hundred acres of tribal trust land. It attracts light industries by offering water, electric, transportation, and communication infrastructure and, uniquely, a 5,700-foot rail line (the A-OK Railroad) that gives assembly, manufacturing, and industrial enterprises direct, low-cost access to the national Union Pacific rail network. The Nation's second investment, not as visible but equally important, was in taking the legal steps in 2014 to secure designation as a foreign trade zone satellite site, which lowers many product costs by reducing duties, tariffs, and regulations. The tribe's decision to take on the Iron Horse project reflected its research findings that potential returns on investment are significantly higher for industrial enterprises than for retail, and that rail transport significantly reduces the cost of heavy freight transport. In choosing to target industry rather than retail, planners also considered the multiplier effect on job creation: one new job in manufacturing creates four to five new jobs—compared to retail, where it takes four jobs to create demand for one more.[4] James Collard, the Nation's director of planning and economic development, points out that planning for Iron Horse included not only projections of income and profit, but also expres-sion of the tribe's vibrant cultural heritage. "Historically, many of the tribes, particularly Citizen Potawatomi Nation, have been traders for hundreds and hundreds of years," he said. "The notion of trade is in the DNA . . . [and the Iron Horse development is] a way to reconnect with that emphasis on trade. . . . It was a good time to fall back on the tribe's roots."[5] Infrastructure improvements empowered the tribal government to attract considerable private investment, which has greatly increased land values, enhanced tribal fiscal self-sufficiency, and created job and business opportunities for their people.

The Choctaw and Potawatomi nations are by no means the only examples of tribes experiencing infrastructure-led growth, but they are among the few. The general condition of infrastructure on reservations throughout the country is at best substandard and at worst abysmal or nonexistent.

The Prevalence of Substandard Tribal Infrastructure

In the early spring of 2020, cases of COVID-19 erupted in the Navajo Nation. Despite a strong tribal government committed to economic development, the tribe struggles to generate revenue, and much of the sprawling reservation lacks even the most basic water and sanitation infrastructure to fight a pandemic. The Centers for Disease Control's urgent recommendation of such simple protections as frequent handwashing to stem COVID-19 transmission was problematic: one-third of the Navajo population has no access to the infrastructure to implement that recommendation. The *Washington Post* reported in December 2019 that nearly one hundred thousand of the reservation's three hundred thousand citizens still have no taps or flushing toilets in their homes and regularly travel long distances to haul water. And the distance is often just one of many problems: "Those who drive miles to windmills, often carrying matches and wood to light fires below the wells' frozen spigots, may draw water that is not safe. Many water sources . . . are marked with signs warning of contamination, some with naturally occurring toxins such as arsenic, some with uranium and other by-products of the mining industry."[6] By May, the Navajo, or the Diné as they call themselves, had the highest COVID infection rate of any population on the continent, surpassing even that of New York City.

Such is the problem of infrastructure in Indian Country, where households are 19 times more likely than White households to lack indoor plumbing.[7] The Indian Health Service estimate for bringing running water and sanitation to the Navajo Reservation is $200 million, and that figure does not include the cost of administrative and jurisdictional problems that compound the shortage of funding. In the southern portion of the reservation, the patch-work of tribal and privately owned parcels that border state and federal lands, known as checkerboarding (see chapter 3), further impedes construction of roads and water lines.[8]

The Navajo Nation is not unique in its infrastructure deficit. The condition and availability of public infrastructure throughout Indian Country stands in stark contrast to that of the rest of the United States. The 2017 NCAI report called out the federal government's dereliction of duty.

> For generations, the federal government—despite abiding trust and treaty obligations—has substantially underinvested in Indian Country's infra-structure, evident in the breadth and severity of its unmet infrastructure needs as compared to the rest of the nation. . . . The number of "shovel ready" infrastructure projects in Indian Country remains too many to count, and many of those have been that way for years if not decades. This chronic underinvestment and the growing backlog of critical infrastruc-ture projects not only negatively impacts the social, physical, and mental wellbeing of Tribal and neighboring communities, it hampers the ability of Tribal Nations to fully leverage their economic potential and the ability of their citizens to fully participate in the American economy.[9]

To put the infrastructure gap in perspective, the NCAI dismissed the $3 billion allocated to Indian Country infrastructure by the American Recovery and Reinvestment Act during the Obama administration as a mere "drop in the bucket" of what it will take to energize self-determined, sustainable community development and economic opportunity in tribal communities.[10]

The examples below, selected from a variety of infrastructure categories addressed in the NCAI report, are indicative of the magnitude of Indian nations' needs:

- *Water.* Compared to 91 percent of the US population, only 88 percent of Native Americans receive water that meets health standards. The estimated need to bring all reservations up to safe drinking-water standards is $45 million annually. In 2016, $20 million was budgeted.
- *Sanitation.* In 2015, 6 percent of American Indian and Alaskan Native homes had no access to sanitation facilities, and the facilities in 47 percent of homes were substandard. The 2016 budget for sanitation facility construction was $99.4 million, as compared to an estimated need of $3.39 billion. The Indian Health Service reported a sanitation-facilities construction backlog of 2,878 projects. The NCAI estimates that tribes receive $4.05 for every $100,000 of need.
- *Dam maintenance and safety.* In 2016, $23.5 million of an estimated $556 million need was budgeted for deferred maintenance on the 137 dams for which the BIA has responsibility. Thirty-one of the dams (located on fifteen reservations) are categorized as "high-significant-hazard," meaning that failure would likely have catastrophic effects, including loss of life, destruction of other public infrastructure, and loss of culture.
- *Electricity.* The 2016 funding of $16.9 million toward an estimated need of $50 million was insufficient to provide basic electric service to the 14.2 percent of tribal households that

must rely on other more expensive and less efficient power sources like gasoline-powered generators. On some reservations, household electricity costs are 275 percent higher than the national average.

- *Transportation infrastructure, BIA roads maintenance.* Average annual funding for what had become by 2016 a $289 million backlog is $24 million.

- *Law enforcement infrastructure.* The NCAI estimated a total need in 2017 of $1 billion, including 4,290 additional officers, noting that 1.3 officers serve every one thousand citizens on tribal lands, as compared to 2.9 officers for every one thousand citizens in non-Indian communities.

- *Communications, broadband, and wireless deployment.* Overall, in 2017, 41 percent of people living on tribal lands (sixteen million total) had no access to broadband or wireless communication. The number rose to 61 percent for rural areas. The national average was 10 percent. Of those who do have access, 43 percent have no choice of provider and pay above-competitive rates because only one company serves their area.[11]

As the above snapshot suggests, the infrastructure necessary to attract investment has not been, and is not likely to be, provided under federal management and transfer financing. If tribal governments want to exercise their sovereignty in the quest for economic renewal, they must develop their own sources of non-transfer-based revenue.

Ideally—though it is unlikely to happen—tribes should continue to receive funding and administrative support throughout the transition to self-administration.

- *Legislative and administrative support.* Federal policy will have to go beyond just allowing tribal governments to exercise self-determination and commit to actively supporting their efforts. Legislation that removes barriers can help tribes build public sectors that can provide and maintain infrastructure, manage land and resources, and meet citizens' demand for education, health, and other social services.

- *Adequate transfer funding.* Tribal governments that choose to assume service responsibilities should receive funding commensurate with their added responsibilities. Funding for services previously provided by the federal bureaucracy should not be reallocated away from self-determining tribes but should flow to their tribal governments. Funding transfers from federal to tribal government should be adequate to ensure service quality comparable to that available to non-Indians without destroying incentives for the tribes to engage in economic development.

- *Direct revenue generation.* Ultimately, economic renewal requires that tribes generate revenue directly to move away from dependence on government transfers. A dependable revenue stream based on a transparent system of taxation and fees not only improves investment climates and business environments but also strengthens incentives for better governance.

Planning Gaps in Tribal Economies

Planning for economic growth is like doing a puzzle with individual projects as the puzzle pieces. One piece might be a road-resurfacing project. Another piece might be upgrading a particular portion of the wastewater collection system. The community's economic development strategy is like the picture on the puzzle box. It represents the tribe's economic goals and guides the manner in which the pieces come together—that is, the order and method of executing the various capital projects. Without the picture on the box, it is difficult to assemble the pieces. A government's capital program often includes a number of projects, but if the program is not integrated with the development strategy, it will lack the management and direction necessary for efficient execution. Development planning without an economic development strategy is tantamount to randomly selecting puzzle pieces from the box and hoping they fit together.

Planning gaps are a major source of weakness in tribal investment climates. One consequence of failure or inability to engage in comprehensive long-term planning is that infrastructure development is piecemeal and uncoordinated. Another is that tribal governments are often unable to work with partners to develop projects of the proper scale and they end up using inappropriate financing tools that result in inefficiencies. And, tribes often encounter large start-up hurdles despite having significant economic development potential. The end result is that property values and rates of investment are much lower than they would be if the infrastructure deficiencies were remedied.

Off-reservation communities typically integrate a number of plans to guide infrastructure provision. The local government generates a land-use plan based on the community's economic goals. A capital plan is then developed to implement the land-use plan and the economic strategy. Next, a capital-financing plan is designed to establish savings or reserve funds for infrastructure construction. Investors are interested in the condition of both existing and probable future infrastructure, so they look for integration of a tribal government's economic development strategy and its capital planning. When these mutually support one another, the stock and quality of infrastructure is likely to improve and with it the ability to attract private investment. Integrated planning is missing or piecemeal in most reservation communities, and few tribal governments have comprehensive economic development strategies as they struggle to meet ongoing needs of their citizens with their limited human resources.

Tribal governments' inexperience with economic planning is not surprising given the legacy of federal management, the inconsistencies of federal policy, and the complexities of tribal politics.

The initiation of policies of self-determination is also burdened by the familiarity of "business as usual." Just as the tribal constitutions written under the tutelage of the BIA mirrored the US Constitution, tribal planning for economic development in the late twentieth and early twenty-first centuries has been shaped by federal funding and federal administrative practice. "When federal agencies were funding motel construction, Native nations built motels; when federal agencies were funding industrial parks, Native nations built industrial parks; if they were funding convenience stores, Native nations built convenience stores."[12] By the 1990s, it had become general practice for tribal councils to hire development planners, most often non-Indians, and task them with unrealistic expectations of overnight results. The 2007 NCAI infrastructure report found that this practice usually resulted in tribal enterprises over which tribal councils exerted inordinate influence in day-to-day operations, policies and practices, and even personnel decisions, to the extent that politics often trumped the pursuit of profit.

> Hire a planner, get a grant, start a business, micromanage the result— these were the key tasks in this approach. It turned out to be a recipe for failure. The reason had little to do with intentions. Both funders and planners in this scenario were trying to meet the needs of Native nations. The issue was the process itself, which had little chance of creating sustainable economies. Burdened by too much federal control, too little strategic thinking, a shortage of business expertise, and an overload of tribal politics, it led to failure after failure across Indian Country.[13]

Successful economic growth requires planning under good leadership with active community participation. When planning begins by identifying and articulating community values, decision making can be based on identified priorities, and resources can be used to further community goals, whether those goals are economic or noneconomic.

Instead of looking for quick fixes or home runs, it focuses on identifying the community's strategic priorities—cultural, political, economic, and social—and on bringing those priorities into day-to-day decision making. If strategic priorities include sustaining particular relationships with the land, what kinds of development policies for land use and related activities will support those relationships? If those priorities include finding ways to sustain seasonal ceremonial cycles while at the same time running competitive enterprises, what sorts of policies will be necessary to do that? . . . [Planned investment] in the physical infrastructure necessary to development . . . [can be accomplished] in ways that respect tribal priorities in areas such as land use, resource protection, and social relationships.[14]

The integration of development goals with respect for culture is on display at Tsigo Bugeh Village. The $5.3 million project of the Ohkay Owingeh (formerly San Juan) Pueblo addresses the need for mixed-income housing, while at the same time evoking the tribe's cultural heritage of communal living. Both goals are identified in the pueblo's master plan for the future, which guides all tribal investment and development. Modeled on the traditional pueblo community structure, Tsigo Bugeh Village consists of attached apartment units situated around two equinox- and solstice-oriented plazas that replicate the historic features of the tribe's original pueblo. Traditional *hornos*, outdoor ovens, are visible in the plazas, and modern amenities—including a community kitchen, business office, and exercise facility—are incorporated into the building structures. The six-and-a-half-acre village has forty rental units, all but nine reserved for pueblo members earning between 40 and 60 percent of the median income in that part of New Mexico. In 2004, the Environmental Protection Agency's National Award for Smart Growth Achievement lauded the integration of economic and cultural goals. Tsigo Bugeh Village "provides a long-term growth strategy, coordinates existing infrastructure with housing and commercial development, preserves the walkable historic plazas, and encourages retail and commercial uses in a 'main street' style. The plan also includes design guidelines that enhance the traditional building pattern to preserve the architectural heritage of the pueblo, fostering a distinctive sense of place."[15]

Comprehensive planning is the essential first step in constructing the foundational public infrastructure that investors expect and routinely find in off-reservation projects. Tsigo Bugeh Village and the Citizen Potawatomi Nation's Iron Horse Industrial Park, discussed earlier, exemplify how governments can close the planning gaps that discourage investment while remaining true to traditional culture.

The tribal public sector bears the responsibility of developing mutually supportive economic strategies that coordinate and inform land-use plans, incorporate capital plans that identify future infrastructure requirements and costs, and propose realistic financing options for the public infrastructure that attracts business.

- *General servicing strategy.* This strategy should address how services can be provided in a cost-effective and efficient manner, and how to balance service demands with affordability. The strategy might address infill versus peripheral development and identify methods to maximize existing service systems.
- *Transportation strategy.* This strategy should address methods to maintain or improve mobility levels while remaining affordable, including but not limited to road construction and community transportation needs.
- *Water system plan.* In addition to water treatment and distribution, the plan might also include conservation measures or emergency supply contingencies.
- *Sanitary sewer system plan.* In addition to collection, treatment, and disposal, the plan may also address specific locational needs like septic fields and tanks, or potential methods of treating and disposing of effluent.

- *Stormwater drainage plan.* This plan should seek to maximize natural drainage patterns and to ensure that development does not interfere with natural watercourses. Drainage infrastructure like detention ponds might be included.
- *Waste management strategy.* This might include landfill sites, compost facilities, education initiatives, and recycling operations.
- *Environmental management strategy.* This may address environmental issues related to climate, energy, air quality, pollution, watershed protection, liquid waste removal, and drinking water.

Capital Financing

The capital-financing portion of an economic plan should identify funding sources (revenue streams) for capital construction projects. Some types of capital infrastructure, like toll roads and water and sewer systems, directly generate revenue through user fees. Others, like local roads and sidewalks, do not. To pay for non-revenue-generating infrastructure, governments typically rely on taxes, fees, and borrowing by issuing municipal bonds. Part of the funding decision depends on whether pay-as-you-go or financing is the better option.

In a pay-as-you-go approach, a capital project is undertaken only after the government has collected enough revenue to pay the full cost. Sources for this approach include current taxes and revenue, funds from capital reserves, special assessments or impact fees, and grants from other governments. There are no interest charges with this approach, but projects cannot be started until the funds are in hand.

With a financing approach, a capital project is paid for before enough revenue has been collected to meet the full cost, and bears the additional cost of interest payments. Typically, this is done by borrowing, in the form of selling bonds that will be paid back over time with taxes, user fee payments, or other revenue sources. This option was first made available as part of self-determination through the Indian Tribal Tax Status Act of 1982, which gave tribal governments the authority to issue tax-exempt bonds for development projects.

To issue bonds, governments must have revenue sources to pay back the bondholders in the future. Nontribal local governments use six vehicles to finance infrastructure: (1) annual property tax and other local revenues, (2) saved local revenues, (3) long-term debentures, (4) development cost charges, (5) public-private partnerships, and (6) transfers from other governments. Multiple sources of revenue enable a local government (sometimes in cooperation with other local governments) to build and maintain the initial infrastructure system and to extend it as needed.

Tribal governments rarely have access to these fiscal tools. Although a small number of tribes have mineral, timber, and energy resource endowments that generate royalties, and some tribal councils collect a portion of tribal enterprise revenue to support tribal government operations, most tribal revenue continues to be federal government transfers through contracts and grants.

Taxation in Indian Country

The biggest impediment to tribes' establishing a dependable tax revenue stream like that enjoyed by state and local governments is jurisdictional ambiguity. As sovereign nations, tribes have the authority to impose taxes on citizens living within reservation boundaries.[16] For practical and legal reasons, most do not. Given the poverty of most reservation populations, income taxes are unlikely to generate much revenue, and property taxes are precluded by the trust status of the majority of reservation land. Taxation of what fee land exists on reservations is a matter of ongoing dispute between tribal and state governments, as are sales, excise, and gross-receipts taxes that can help pay for public services from which businesses would benefit. Conflict with state and local governments over taxation means that most tribal governments must look to other sources if they wish to self-fund public services and infrastructure to attract investment.[17]

Until the 1970s, federal policy was not designed to promote development of independent Indian governments and vibrant economies. Consequently, tribes choosing to actively pursue self-determination found themselves without many of the tools available to nontribal governments—notably the power to generate revenue through taxation. In simplest terms, the problem has been and continues to be that the federal government will not give a definitive answer to the question of who has fiscal power in Indian Country. In the absence of legislative direction, the courts have generated many, often conflicting, answers—which is tantamount to no answer at all. Given the uncertainty, it is not surprising that tribes' efforts to assert fiscal authority are routinely challenged by state and local governments.

Taxing authority in Indian Country derives from the Constitution and from Supreme Court decisions that affirm the power of Congress to regulate Indian affairs and of the federal executive branch to administer legislated policy. Within that framework, federal tax jurisdiction over tribes and their citizens is well-established, but state and local authority are not. While it might seem that the supremacy of the federal government preempts state and local governments from taxing tribes, tribal enterprises, and tribal property, in practice the lines of jurisdiction are persistently unclear. With much revenue at stake and the outcome of litigation unpredictable, state and local governments have strong incentives to challenge tribal jurisdiction and assert their own. The resulting litigation is costly, frustrates tribal governments, and weakens investment climates.

More than forty years ago, Supreme Court Justice William Rehnquist observed, "Since early in the last century, this Court has been struggling to develop a coherent doctrine by which to measure with some predictability the scope of Indian immunity from state taxation."[18] The struggle continues. While repeatedly chiding Congress for its failure to legislate rules for determining if and when state taxes and fees can be applied to Indian tribes or their citizens, the Court has adopted a case-by-case approach that attempts to balance federal and tribal interests against those of the state involved in the dispute. Called Bracker tests, from the Court's 1980 decision in *White Mountain Apache Tribe v. Bracker*, these balancing tests are notoriously unpredictable and their decisions rarely transferable. As the Native Nations Institute observes, requiring case-by-case evaluation "rarely leads to comprehensive, predictable, or transferrable solutions to the issues that arise between tribes and neighboring state and local governments. Court rulings in Indian tax litigation regularly create more uncertainties than they resolve." The Institute's 2016 analysis concludes that "the harm done to tribal *and state* governments and their citizens by unpredictable and incoherent tax policy is real: Dollars and time are wasted, resources go untapped, government-to-government relationships fester and break down, and absurdities in business development practices prevail. . . . Economic development that should occur does not."[19]

Establishing a tax-based revenue stream is complicated, ironically, by the unclear limits of tribal governments' authority to exempt businesses from taxation, a strategy used frequently by state and local governments to fund public infrastructure. While potentially a powerful development tool, tribal economic development bonds, like other federal tax-incentive policies, have proven not to be major attractors of new business or a benefit to tribally owned businesses, again underscoring the urgency of empowering tribal governments by clarifying the extent and limits of state, local, and tribal fiscal authority.[20]

Dual Taxation

The specter of dual taxation—that a business could be taxed by the tribe and by the state in which the reservation lies—is threatening enough that the American Bar Association warns its member attorneys to do their homework before advising clients contracting for work in Indian Country. For those tempted to dismiss the warning, the Association provides a simple example of how failure to identify all taxing authorities within reservation boundaries can turn profits into losses. A construction company working on the Navajo Reservation on a road project contract with the Bureau of Indian Affairs knew that it was required to pay the 3 percent gross-receipts tax imposed by the Navajo Nation. Accordingly, it took account of that in its pricing. Since the work was on the reservation and was for the federal government, the company erroneously assumed that it would be exempt from New Mexico's 6 percent gross-receipts tax, even though the project was located completely within the state's boundaries, and did not account for that cost in its bid for the project. In a competitive environment, paying New Mexico's 6 percent tax would gobble up the company's profit.[21]

Law and precedent are clear that states are preempted from imposing any tax in which the incidence would fall on a tribe, tribal citizens, or tribal enterprises. Thus, state governments may not tax income that tribal citizens earn on their reservations, nor tax sales by tribal corporations to tribal citizens, nor levy property taxes on reservation trust lands. This sovereign jurisdiction of tribal governments over their own citizens is rarely disputed. The contentious issue is whether state and local governments have the authority to tax nontribal state citizens' economic transactions on reservations and compel reservation businesses to collect the tax. Outside Indian Country, with few exceptions, state and local governments cannot tax their citizens or enterprises doing business in other states, but that principle has not been definitively established with regard to state and local citizens doing business on Indian reservations, regardless of whether the tribe itself imposes a tax. The catch-22 for tribal governments is that if they do not tax sales, they give up revenue, but if they do impose a tax and dual taxation ensues, economic activity stalls and the goal of establishing an effective revenue stream remains unfulfilled. Navajo Nation President Peterson Zah made clear in testimony to Congress that tribal governments are keenly aware of cost imposed on Indian economies by the no-win rules of the game: "Double taxation interferes with our ability to encourage economic activity and to develop effective revenue generating tax programs. Many businesses may find it easier to avoid doing business on our reservations rather than . . . bear the brunt of an added tax burden" (as cited in *Michigan v. Bay Mills Indian Community*, 2014).[22]

Even with careful planning, it is hard for tribes to avoid dual taxation. Great Wolf Resorts Inc. partnered with the Confederated Tribes of the Chehalis Reservation to build a water park, resort, and conference center on tribal trust land. The partnership took great pains to secure BIA approval of the lease and to draft a business plan minimizing state and local taxes; it even went so far as to secure a Washington State Department of Revenue ruling formally establishing an exemption from state taxes. A year later, the partnership was blindsided when, despite the ruling, the county assessed property taxes. Although the tribe eventually prevailed (*Chehalis Tribes v. Thurston County*), it suffered five years of costly litigation because of the uncertainty that incentivized the county's action.[23]

The potential time and cost of tax litigation carries inordinate weight in tribal economic decision making, often to the point of eclipsing sound business practices and policies that would be prioritized in the absence of the litigation threat. When choosing between alternatives, tribes consider the likelihood of the state suit and of the tribe prevailing in court. Litigation avoidance also strongly influences decisions about the location, business structure, and products of tribal enterprises. Suppose a tribe's goal is to increase revenue for public services and infrastructure with a sales tax, and it is considering two locations for a new commercial enterprise, one on trust land and one on fee land. The advantage of selecting the trust parcel is that the tribe is more likely to survive a Bracker balancing test challenge of its right to preempt state sales taxes to non-Indian customers. Given the atmosphere of judicial uncertainty, this advantage tends to prevail even if the fee parcel has better roads and better water, sewage, and public service infrastructure, and is more easily accessible to customers. The trust advantage is large enough that tribes with little trust land often choose to petition the federal government for approval to transfer fee land they have purchased into trust, even though that process can be expensive and uncertain and can delay development for years.[24]

The threat of tax litigation also keeps Indian economies from healthy diversification of products. Tobacco, gasoline, and fireworks sales and casino gambling are common on reservations precisely because they are either prohibited or heavily taxed by nearby states to the point that customers are attracted by the lower prices on reservations. Marijuana is a relatively new addition to this category. The Pyramid Lake Paiute Tribe, located in Nevada where marijuana is legal, sells pot near the Las Vegas Strip, and other tribes in marijuana-legal states are considering following suit in their tourist centers. In March 2020, the Oglala Sioux Tribe on the Pine Ridge Reservation voted to legalize recreational and medical marijuana, although it is prohibited in South Dakota and other nearby states. To address the state's concerns, the Oglala have taken on the cost of enforcing the state's law that customers may not take pot off the reservation. Legalization for medical and recreational uses was approved in November 2020 elections in South Dakota, and the tribe expects to be well positioned to compete with off-reservation suppliers. Tribal planners are also aware that diversification requires more than adding another product to the line of tax-free items, so they intend to capitalize on South Dakota's significant tourist trade by building a marijuana resort near the tribal casino in the Black Hills.[25]

Tribal Development Benefits with Off-Reservation Economies

Policy makers who insist on asserting state taxing authority hold the mistaken notion that successful tribal enterprises reduce income and employment in nearby off-reservation communities. This misunderstanding presumes that economic growth is a zero-sum game in which the gains of a tribal economy must be losses for the state economy. To the contrary, the size of the economic "pie" is not fixed, and both state and tribe can benefit from tribal economic development. Like many others, the state of Washington maintains that Indian economic growth causes fiscal damage to the state. The folly of that belief lies in ignoring the degree to which tribal development projects depend on materials, supplies, and labor that are not produced on the reservation. The Tulalip Tribes buy more than 90 percent of resources, goods, and services from off-reservation businesses—all of whom pay property and sales taxes, as do their employees (who also pay income taxes in some states).[26]

The story of Quil Ceda Village exemplifies the shortsightedness of Washington legislators' zero-sum thinking. This commercial center was built by the Tulalip Tribes on a strip of reservation land that contained only an abandoned industrial building once leased to Boeing Airlines. The Tribes invested in infrastructure, chartered the municipality under federal law, and commissioned a governing body to provide oversight and administer leases to companies like Home Depot, Cabela's, and Walmart, all lured by the Interstate 5 corridor location. The Village draws tens of thousands of customers yearly and employs more than one thousand people, the majority non-Indian.

Quil Ceda is hugely successful, but for years the tribes' only return on investment was lease revenue. Washington State's assertion of tax authority denied tribal government access to a direct revenue stream that could fund future development. The loss was not insignificant. In 2016, the state collected $27 million and Snohomish County collected $9 million in sales tax. The abandoned and deteriorating Boeing facility and vacant land were, in effect, dead capital that the tribal government revived, but it could not capture the revenue its investment generated.

Tulalip Tribal Board Chair Teri Gobin expressed the frustration that led to the tribe's filing suit. "For 20-plus years, the Tribe has attempted to get both the State and County to enter into a tax compact to share some of the tax revenues generated within Quil Ceda Village. . . . To date, we have never received a dollar, yet we have been 100 percent responsible for the costs of all the infrastructure and governmental services that allow those businesses to operate."[27]

The five-year litigation, in which the tribe was backed by the US Department of Justice, ended in January 2020, preempted by a negotiated agreement among the state, county, and tribe. The Tulalip agreed to build a $35 million civil-commitment mental health center in Snohomish County in return for a share of state sales tax collected at Quil Ceda. The tribe's share is estimated to exceed $30 million annually by 2025. In March 2020, the governor signed legislation allowing tax-sharing compacts with federally recognized tribes, legitimizing the agreement. The state trumpets its "groundbreaking" model for revenue sharing, but it remains to be seen if other states are persuaded of the benefits and willing to abandon the beggar-thy-neighbor approach to Indian economic development.

Despite the accumulating evidence, there are presently few state and local governments that recognize the significant off-reservation benefits of supporting Indian economic development. North Dakota's beggar-thy-neighbor stance toward the Mandan, Hidatsa, and Arikara (MHA) Nation remains more common than Nevada's active partnership with the Reno-Sparks tribe. By 2015, fossil fuel production on the MHA's Fort Berthold reservation had generated a $3.3 billion surplus for the state government of North Dakota, but when energy development damaged roads, increased traffic fatalities, and caused an upsurge in crime, North Dakota turned a blind eye to the harms inflicted on reservation residents, energy producers, and energy workers. In 2011, despite having collected $82 million from energy production, the state budgeted only $2 million for state highway repair and maintenance, and $0 for BIA and tribal road repair and maintenance. Concerned about time loss and equipment damage in an industry with low profit margins, energy companies felt they had no choice but to maintain the roads themselves, despite not having agreed to do so in their contracts with the state.

When the companies petitioned state policy makers to increase infrastructure funding and to address the impact of the rapid influx of workers on reservation housing and on emergency, health, and social services, Ron Ness, president of the North Dakota Petroleum Council, warned, to little effect, that the tremendous wealth potential of developing the state's oil-rich Bakken Formation was endangered by the intransigent disregard for the needs of the MHA Nation and by the state's unwillingness to fulfill its responsibility for infrastructure maintenance on and off the reservation. "There is an incredible opportunity resulting from oil and gas production for all North Dakota citizens, including those living on Fort Berthold. The availability of increased funding will help the MHA Nation *meet* their *infrastructure* needs, will provide *benefits to the surrounding communities* and provide important assurance that North Dakota continues to be a state that provides *opportunity and fair treatment for all its citizens.*"[28]

In contrast to North Dakota, Nevada state government has positioned itself to share in the benefits of economic diversification by the Reno-Sparks Indian Colony. In 1989, the state enacted legislation that prevents it from collecting sales tax if a tribe files its own tribal sales tax ordinance with the Nevada Department of Taxation, and if the tribal tax is equal to or greater than the state sales tax. The Reno-Sparks tribal government quickly took advantage of the opportunity—and to good effect. To break its complete dependence on tobacco sales revenue, the tribe decided to include commercial leasing and development, earning revenue from big tenants like Walmart and car dealerships and from a growing number of small local businesses, all commercial enterprises that employ many non-Indian workers. Nevada benefits further from the tribe's participation in partnerships with nearby companies and local governments. The tribe has opened a health clinic that serves nonmember Indians who would otherwise depend on local and state government health services.[29]

Revising the Indian Trader Regulations and Shaping the Regulatory Environment

Over the past fifty years, the Supreme Court has renewed its urging that Congress enact legislation to definitively establish the fiscal and regulatory jurisdictions of tribal and state governments. The Indian Trader regulations, first enacted in 1834 and last amended in 1957, placed fiscal responsibility for Indian tribes exclusively on the federal government, giving it scope in regulating Indian economic activity and in determining who is allowed to do business with the tribes. The text of 25 U.S.C. 262 states: "Any person desiring to trade with the Indians on any Indian reservation shall, upon establishing the fact, to the satisfaction of the Commissioner of Indian Affairs, that he is a proper person to engage in such trade, be permitted to do so under such rules and regulations as the Commissioner of Indian Affairs may prescribe for the protection of said Indians." The paternalism of the regulation, despite its intention to protect

Indian tribes from White exploitation, stands in clear opposition to the goals of contemporary self-determination policy.

With the support of the NCAI, the BIA has proposed revisions to the Indian Trader statutes that resolve this conflict by empowering tribes to shape their own economies and clearing up the jurisdictional uncertainties that incentivize litigation. The proposed revisions would vest tribal government with regulatory and licensing authority, preempt all state taxation except in negotiated agreement with tribal governments, eliminate balancing tests, and establish tribal courts as the default venue for commercial dispute resolution in the absence of a formal agreement designating another court or regulatory body. To date, the reformers have been no more successful than the Supreme Court in moving Congress. Its refusal to act perpetuates uncertainty and continues to impede Indian nations' economic development.[30]

Governments at all levels design regulatory environments to attract investment. Accordingly, tribal governments' authority over their regulatory environments could be a powerful tool for councils to encourage entrepreneurial ventures and generate the capital investment necessary to execute them. Shaping the regulatory environment can also help to attract investment in development projects.

The Native Nations Institute outlines several components that are necessary for creating a safe, business-friendly regulatory environment:

- Transparent, straightforward, and timely business-licensing requirements
- Clear zoning rules that set aside land for commercial purposes
- Streamlined and fair leasing procedures
- Strong rules to prevent political interference in business processes
- Policies that allow limited waivers of sovereign immunity[31]

By adopting licensing procedures that are transparent, influence-free, and timely, self-determination allows tribal governments to reclaim the power to decide who may do business on reservations, a power that had been preempted by the Indian Trader regulations. To attract investment, licensing must be uncomplicated and, where beneficial to the tribal community, less onerous than that required by off-reservation jurisdictions. Requiring periodic license renewal provides a relatively low-cost way to check whether businesses adhere to tribal laws; comply with commercial, building, and land-use codes; possess required tribal permits; and collect and submit tribal sales taxes and fees. The Native Nations Institute points out that, in addition to supporting economic renewal, business licensing can also be a powerful tool for preserving culture and tradition. Heritage can be safeguarded by, for example, certifying the authenticity of tribal artists, or by defining the approved and prohibited commercial uses of cultural symbols and artifacts, dances, ceremonies, and songs. Tribes can also make the investment climate less precarious by limiting their own actions, not only through negotiated sovereign immunity waivers, but also by adopting and rigorously enforcing prohibitions of political interference in licensing, code compliance, and other commercial regulations.[32]

Used judiciously, regulatory power can be transformative. Kayenta is now a vibrant town of 5,200 in the Navajo Nation, but as recently as the 1980s, it was severely impoverished and most residents were unemployed. The investment climate was dreary and cost-heavy; public infrastructure was substandard or nonexistent; and the business environment was burdened by arcane and ultimately stultifying permitting and licensing procedures. Securing project approval from the tribal government in Window Rock required round trips of three hundred miles over poorly constructed and haphazardly maintained reservation roads. Coming together, Kayenta residents decided that only local control would give them any chance of economic renewal. In 1985, the Navajo Nation

Council granted their petition for township status, which gave the community a municipal government with increased power to craft local regulations. Community leaders moved quickly to reshape the regulatory framework by simplifying licensing, permitting, and development-approval procedures; adopting straightforward building and commercial codes; and instituting a 2.5 percent sales tax. As revenue came in over the following decade, Kayenta's public infrastructure was transformed by improvements to drainage and flood control, fire and police protection, street construction and maintenance, and water and sewage systems. Its efforts to jump-start the virtuous circle of investment paid off. Today, restaurants and hotels, entertainment venues, small professional and retail businesses, a grocery store, and gas stations are evidence that the improved regulatory environment is attracting investment and revitalizing a once lifeless economy.[33]

Funding Infrastructure without Tax Revenue

Given the improbability that taxation will soon become a viable source of direct revenue to fund public infrastructure, tribal governments are experimenting with alternatives. Among the most promising are service agreements and community development financing, both of which have features that call on cooperative and communal traditions common to many Native Americans' tribal heritage.

Service Agreements

Potential investors, including commercial and residential developers, home buyers, and lenders, want to know how water, sewers and sewage treatment, roads and road maintenance, parks, garbage collection, snow removal, and police and fire protection will be provided and what fees and taxes they may have to pay, now and in the future, to ensure ongoing provision and maintenance. Unable to establish the dependable direct revenue streams that would allay investors' concerns, some tribes are turning to negotiated service agreements with nearby local governments. A service agreement is a contractual relationship between two governments for the provision of services and sharing of physical infrastructure. The agreement specifies what local services and infrastructure each government will provide, how they will be provided, who will pay, and a formula for calculating payment. Some of the most common shared services are water and sewage treatment, education, and fire protection. Such agreements can significantly boost investor confidence regarding the quality, continuity, and pricing of local services within a region, and they have the added benefit of encouraging expanded government-to-government cooperation in such areas as region-wide capital planning, land-use planning, economic development planning, and uniformity of protocols and regulatory standards.

Schooling is a common first venture in service agreements. Shifting population patterns in communities bordering reservations may leave school districts with excess capacity in the form of empty schools and unused recreation facilities, and leave reservation children who attended those now-closed schools with only costly or inconvenient alternatives. In such situations, it is often possible to reach mutually beneficial agreements with little money changing hands. A case in point is the $1 yearly lease the Pascua Yaqui Tribe has paid the Tucson Unified School District since 2014 to use the building and grounds of Richey Elementary School, which the district had closed. Many Pascua Yaqui children had attended Richey Elementary, and the school closure was a blow to them and their families. District leaders were sympathetic to the tribe's educational needs and entered into negotiations with the tribal council. Once satisfied that the Pascua Yaqui's insurance would cover the tribal volunteers and staff, who would all be subject to background checks, the school district was willing to approve the lease. Although the district receives only $1 per year, it has been happily freed of the responsibility for utilities and maintenance of the school buildings and facilities, including a gym and an auditorium, playing fields, and outdoor courts. For their part, the Pascua Yaqui have not only gained control of their children's education but have been able to expand the public services available to all tribal members. The leased school facility accommodates sports leagues, hosts job fairs, and offers recreational classes and tournaments for teens. Currently, tribal leaders are responding to the desire for workout space and equipment that was expressed in a community survey. Plans for the future include providing health and dental care on the school site.[34]

As the practice of sharing services spreads, tribes and bordering communities are experiencing both near- and long-term benefits.

- *Lower costs.* Together, the combined service populations of the tribal and local governments are larger than those of each alone. Savings occur when the cost of servicing an additional taxpayer decreases as the number of taxpayers increases. This is usually true for any service with large fixed or initial costs, such as sewer or water services. Once the infrastructure is in place, the cost of adding another user is very low. Both parties to the agreement benefit; the government providing the service gains revenue, and the government purchasing the service avoids the large front-end costs.
- *Access to capital infrastructure.* Traditionally, local governments have had greater access to financing than have tribes. Local governments near reservation boundaries likely have significant capital infrastructure already in place along with the skills, people, and equipment to maintain it. In some cases, the costs per taxpayer would be so high that the project would not be feasible for the tribe alone.
- *Less duplication.* Service agreements allow governments to make more efficient use of existing services and to reduce the environmental impact of infrastructure duplication. A good

example of this is the agreement between the Oneida Nation of Wisconsin and the village of Ashwaubenon, the boundaries of which overlap. To jointly meet the federal requirements for stormwater management, the village provided the infrastructure, and the tribe shares in operating and maintenance costs for the treatment facility. Ashwaubenon charges the Oneida Nation in proportion to its share of the contributory flow, discounted based on the tribe's continued maintenance of a small treatment pond on the reservation. The potential problems of dual taxation are avoided by the village agreeing not to levy assessments on fee land within the reservation boundaries. In return, the tribe pays the cost of street improvements and maintenance, including grading, graveling, paving, and repair of any streets, on or off the reservation, that benefit reservation residents. Under the current agreement, the tribe also pays the village approximately $300,000 annually for fire, police, and trash services.[35] A good deal that cuts costs for both communities, the service agreement substitutes cooperation for jurisdictional conflict.

- *Utilization of excess capacity.* When a local government builds capital infrastructure or acquires the capacity to provide a service, it usually ends up with excess capacity, partly to accommodate future growth and partly due to the indivisibility of some components. For example, a town with a population of twenty-five thousand may build water supply infrastructure to meet the needs of a population of fifty thousand. Or, a town may hire a full-time animal control officer and build a pound facility when it only needs animal control services three days a week—but the impounded animals have to be cared for seven days a week. Selling water or animal control services to the neighboring tribe rids the local government of excess capacity and increases revenues while sparing the tribe the construction cost of separate facilities.

- *Positive relationships.* By addressing areas of common concern and future opportunity, service agreements can be a major building block in developing and strengthening a positive relationship between local and tribal governments. With an agreement, the parties form a larger community signaling that they want to work together well into the future in a spirit of cooperation.

Community Development Financial Institutions

Another option for tribes that cannot establish a direct revenue stream through taxation is to use community development financial institutions, or CDFIs, to fund infrastructure. CDFIs are locally controlled, nonprofit lending organizations designed to stimulate economic growth in low-income communities with little or no access to banks and other traditional lenders. They are privately owned and privately funded by individuals, corporations, religious organizations, and other nonprofits, and they are administered by the US Department of the Treasury. Because CDFIs typically have more flexible lending practices than traditional banks and other financial institutions, they can be especially important sources for tribal governments struggling to fund physical infrastructure.[36]

The US Treasury designation "Native CDFI" applies only to institutions conducting half or more of their business with Native Americans, Native Hawaiians, and Native Alaskans. In 2009, the Native CDFI Network was founded to coordinate and support the seventy-three (out of approximately one thousand) CDFIs that are Native. The Network strives "to be a national voice and advocate that strengthens and promotes Native Community development financial institutions, creating access to capital and resources for Native peoples. Its webinars, listening sessions, industry meetings, and advocacy promote peer-to-peer networking, the dissemination of best practices, and a platform from which the Native CDFI voice can be heard."[37]

To provide the needed community-tailored loan products, Native CDFIs face two significant challenges—to accumulate sufficient financial resources and to acquire or develop the human capital to organize, administer, and monitor a wide variety of financial services and lending products. The Oweesta Corporation, itself a CDFI, has amassed a pool of over $10 million to fund other members of the CDFI Native Network.[38] Although loans are typically small in comparison to those made by off-reservation financial institutions, they can make the difference in individuals' well-being and thereby strengthen tribal economies. The Four Bands Community Fund was started in 2000 to serve the Cheyenne River Sioux Tribe in South Dakota, and like many Native CDFIs, it offers both loan products and services—like financial education, business coaching, tax preparation, and credit-builder programs—designed to empower tribal citizens to actively engage in both on- and off-reservation economies. To succeed in their community-focused mission, CDFIs must be more nimble than traditional lending institutions. The ability to respond quickly proves especially valuable in emergencies, such as the one that occurred in the fall of 2013 when an unseasonal blizzard killed hundreds of cattle on the Cheyenne River Reservation. The congressional budget deadlock had closed the usual federal sources of aid, but the Four Bands Community Fund stepped into the breach right away, issuing fifty-eight emergency loans, totaling $128,977, to ranchers and to furloughed government employees.[39]

The community focus of Native CDFIs promotes thinking outside the box or, in the case of the Oglala Sioux Tribe in Pine Ridge, South Dakota, thinking outside the traditional brick-and-mortar financial institution. The First Peoples Fund was established to foster the unique economic potential of Pine Ridge residents, a potential the fund identified through direct observation and survey. The survey revealed that more than 50 percent of Pine Ridge households had some sort of home-based business, that 79 percent of those businesses were arts based, and that more than 60 percent of the would-be artist-entrepreneurs earned less than $10,000 annually. Fund members were convinced that training workshops could greatly increase potential earnings but realized that the expanse of the reservation was a significant hurdle. Undeterred, First Peoples decided that "if they can't come to us, we'll go to them," and Rolling Rez Arts was born.[40] The mobile Rolling Rez Arts unit, a converted airport shuttle bus, provides workshops, financial and entrepreneurship classes, and banking services, and it has the capability to stream video from art conferences and festivals. Some days, the shuttle sports a "Buying Art Today" sign, has buyers and dealers on board, and heads to locations accessible to artists who cannot leave their herds or do not have cars. A $100,000 grant from the National Endowment for the Humanities and the Corporation for Public Broadcasting in 2017 recognized the success of Rolling Rez Arts and allowed it to expand the rolling schedule to the Standing Rock and Cheyenne River Sioux reservations.

Conclusion

Fiscal and financial institutions are integral to the economic transformation of tribal nations. The rules of the game have the power to open financial access to individual citizens, strengthen tribal governments, and encourage on- and off-reservation investment of time, creativity, and resources in productive, future-directed activity while honoring culture and tradition. Unfortunately, fiscal power and access to financial resources are missing from the recipe for development in Indian Country.

There is reason for hope, however, in the growing number of tribes and individual Indian citizens taking steps toward replacing a federal-government-grant-based economy with a productive revenue-based economy. Success varies, of course, and many Indian nations and people remain stuck in transfer-dependent poverty, but by the early 2000s stories of increased economic autonomy and diversification were being told. In 2007, the NCAI expressed confidence in emerging evidence that

> most Native nation economies are now involved in . . . transformation in one way or another, and it appears to be gathering steam. . . . Patterns of revenue-generation look very different today. Nation-owned enterprises are on the rise. Many are responses not to outside agendas but to tribal agendas, and many are generating significant revenues. Citizen entrepreneurship also is on the rise. . . . As economic activity starts to reflect nation-identified assets and priorities and citizen initiatives, reservation economies start to diverge from each other. This same transformation is also restoring to native Nations a dramatically increased measure of control over how they support themselves, something lost to most of these nations in the massive nineteenth-century expropriation of indigenous lands and related resources.[41]

Institutional fiscal and financial change is making economic renewal possible.

EPILOGUE

The preceding chapters have a common theme: American Indians, and indeed Indigenous peoples around the world, created viable, sophisticated institutions that promoted prosperity. With those institutions in place, they did not just survive—they thrived, meeting and often exceeding the living standards of their contemporaries in Europe. The message of this book is that they can thrive again—by shrugging off the burden of stereotype that labels them incompetent, robs them of energy and creativity, and condemns them to a future of dependent poverty. It bears emphasizing over and over again that the history of Indigenous peoples in the Americas is replete with examples of their understanding that specialization and trade create wealth and of their ability to adapt their institutions to the changing conditions of their environments.

Long before European contact, American Indians created incentive-compatible institutions, adopting both formal and informal "rules of the game" that encouraged investment and rewarded productivity with increased bounty and well-being. Those institutions reveal their sophistication and the ability of tribes to adapt. The hunt leader who organized a buffalo drive over a piskun, for example, obtained his skills through significant investment in observing buffalo behavior and analyzing grazing and migration patterns.

He also invested in his own leadership skills so that he could organize hide-covered hunters to lead the buffalo into drivelines and instill in those behind the drive cairns the discipline to stand their ground in the face of huge, stampeding beasts. From the time they were young girls, Indian women invested in developing skills to preserve copious amounts of meat; to locate and remember the whereabouts of productive berry, nut, and seed patches; and to use animal hides and native vegetation to create shelter and clothing.

With the arrival of Europeans, American Indian institutions not only remained viable, they evolved and adapted. With amazing quickness, the Plains tribes adopted the horse to gain advantage in war, to hunt buffalo more effectively, and to transport themselves, their homes, and their goods. The reward for the hunter who invested in training this valuable new asset was the first choice of meat from a successful hunt, a claim he could confidently assert because his property—the uniquely painted arrows or lance found in the kill—verified his right. A woman's property rights were recognized, too; the highly valued tipis she produced by tanning and piecing together hides were acknowledged to be hers. Women also invested in new skills and activities. When Europeans paid for furs with glass beads, women developed new art forms and some began to specialize, trading their beading skills for food, horses, or other valued items. Trade within tribes, villages, or clans quickly expanded to include others, and indeed, trade goods often traveled farther and faster than the Europeans who brought them.

The ability to innovate, adapt, and shape institutions, even throughout the period of colonization, continued, against all odds, into the reservation period, as some tribes showed their resilience and ingenuity. The Blackfeet, for example, who were accustomed to communal tending of horses, quickly became communal cattle herders. Like horses, cattle were owned by individuals or clans but herded jointly. Not only did their success make them self-sufficient, it allowed them to profit by selling beef to the Great Northern Railway, which was being built through their territory.

American Indians were innovative, prosperous, and resilient.

The preceding chapters also make it clear—the Blackfeet and select others notwithstanding—that the top-down institutions adopted by the US government and imposed on Indian nations ignored and overrode the viable, resilient, and adaptable institutions that had served American Indians well. Wardship and trusteeship thwarted and continue to thwart innovation, ingenuity, and in many cases the very viability of American Indian cultures and communities. At its best, trusteeship ensured that not all of Indian Country was transferred to non-Indians, but at its worst, and more commonly, the US government's preemption of the right to decide whether or not individuals are "competent and capable" has proven inimical to both freedom and prosperity.

American Indians were deprived of their freedom to be innovative, prosperous, and resilient.

As the examples throughout this book testify, the potential for freedom and prosperity still exists, but the path forward requires initiative by Indians for Indians. In the words of Crow tribal member Bill Yellowtail, "We must give Indians permission to pursue that age-old but newly remembered paradigm of entrepreneurial self-sufficiency. Surely that is not the entire solution, but it is part of the puzzle."[1]

Around the country and throughout the world, Indigenous peoples are demonstrating the ability to renew their economies and adopt modern business practices within the frameworks of their traditional cultures. Tribes are turning their resources—casinos; recreation and tourism opportunities; oil, gas, and coal reserves; soybean farms; and wildlife—into assets. These they husband

and reinvest: the Southern Utes, for example, turning oil and gas revenues into reservation infrastructure and off-reservation real estate; the Coushatta Tribe of Louisiana allocating some casino revenues to farming enterprises and to forging a trade agreement with Israel. The stories told here of the Southern Utes, the Coushatta, the Citizen Band Potawatomi, the Ohkay Owingeh Pueblo, the Tulalip Tribes, the Wisconsin Oneida Nation, the Pequot Tribe, the Viejas Band of Kumeyaay Indians, and others testify to the real potential for American Indians to reestablish control of their economic well-being by building on the institutional foundations of their cultural heritage.

As the successes, small and large, illustrate, the way to a prosperous future is neither easy nor quick. Taking on the challenge demands persistent vigilance and commitment to maintaining incentive-compatible institutions capable of spawning innovation, generating entrepreneurship, and encouraging trade. The success stories also point out that maintaining a wealth-creating institutional structure requires attention, not just to productivity and trade but also to the organization of tribal government structures, to the accountability of tribal leaders, to the maintenance of modern accounting records, and to the nurturing of individual entrepreneurship. Despite these challenges, the success stories told here herald hope and possibility and make it clear that American Indians are, indeed, both "competent and capable" of renewing their economies.

American Indians can and will renew their economies based on cultural traditions and sound tribal institutions.

NOTES

Prologue

1. Dedrick Asante Muhammad, Rogelio Tec, and Kathy Ramirez, "Racial Wealth Snapshot: American Indians / Native Americans," National Community Reinvestment Coalition, November 18, 2019.
2. Sally C. Curtin and Holly Hedegaard, "Suicide Rates for Females and Males by Race and Ethnicity: United States, 1999 and 2017," Centers for Disease Control and Prevention, updated June 20, 2019.
3. Garet Bleir and Anya Zoledziowski, "Murdered and Missing Native American Women Challenge Police and Courts," Center for Public Integrity, updated October 29, 2018.
4. "Democracy Index 2019," Economist Intelligence Unit, https://www.eiu.com/n/campaigns/democracy-index-2019/.

Chapter 1

1. Daron Acemoglu, Simon Johnson, and James A. Robinson, "Reversal of Fortune: Geography and Institutions in the Making of the Modern World Income Distribution," *Quarterly Journal of Economics* 117, no. 4 (2002): 1231–94.
2. See Naomi Schaefer Riley, *The New Trail of Tears: How Washington Is Destroying American Indians* (New York: Encounter Books, 2016).
3. Charles C. Mann, *1491: New Revelations of the Americas Before Columbus* (New York: Vintage Books, 2006), 143.
4. Mann, 50.
5. Mann, 51.
6. Mann, 51.
7. Mann, 58.
8. Mann, 66.
9. Mann, 58.

10. Manny Jules, foreword to *Beyond the Indian Act: Restoring Aboriginal Property Rights*, by Tom Flanagan, Christopher Alcantara, and Andre Le Dressay (Montreal: McGill-Queen's University Press, 2010), viii–ix.
11. Jules in *Beyond the Indian Act*, ix, xiii.
12. See Douglass C. North, *Institutions, Institutional Change, and Economic Performance* (Cambridge: Cambridge University Press, 1990).
13. Pekka Hämäläinen, *Lakota America: A New History of Indigenous Power* (New Haven, CT: Yale University Press, 2019).
14. Jonathan Lear, *Radical Hope: Ethics in the Face of Cultural Devastation* (Cambridge, MA: Harvard University Press, 2006), 13.
15. Ted Perry, "Chief Seattle's Speech," Center for the Study of the Pacific Northwest, from film script for *Home* (Southern Baptist Radio and Television Commission, 1972), reprinted in Rudolf Kaiser, "Chief Seattle's Speech(es): American Origins and European Reception," in *Recovering the Word: Essays on Native American Literature*, ed. Brian Swann and Arnold Krupat (Berkeley: University of California Press, 1987), 525–30.
16. Paul S. Wilson, "What Chief Seattle Said," *Environmental Law* 22, no. 4 (1992), 1457.
17. Robert J. Miller, *Reservation "Capitalism": Economic Development in Indian Country* (Lincoln: University of Nebraska Press, 2013), 27.
18. Mann, *1491*, 46.
19. Terry L. Anderson and Wilcomb E. Washburn, *Sovereign Nations or Reservations: An Economic History of American Indians* (San Francisco: Pacific Research Institute for Public Policy, 1995), 38.
20. Flanagan, Alcantara, and Le Dressay, *Beyond the Indian Act*, 34.
21. Judith Williams, *Clam Gardens: Aboriginal Mariculture on Canada's West Coast* (Vancouver, BC: New Star Books, 2006).
22. Florence Hawley Ellis, "Isleta Pueblo," in *Handbook of North American Indians*, vol. 9 (Washington, DC: Smithsonian Institution, 1979), 355.
23. Adam Smith, *An Inquiry into the Nature and Causes of the Wealth of Nations*, ed. Edwin A. Seligman (London: J. M. Dent, 1901), 12–15, 400–401, 436–37.
24. George Colvin, "The Presence, Source and Use of Fossil Shark Teeth from Ohio Archaeological Sites," *Ohio Archaeologist* 61, no. 4 (Fall 2011).
25. M. Hirch, "Trading across Time and Space: Culture along the North American 'Grease Trails' from a European Perspective," presentation at Thompson Rivers University, Kamloops, British Columbia, 2003, quoted in André Le Dressay, Normand Lavallee, and Jason Reeves, "First Nations Trade, Specialization, and Market Institutions: A Historical Survey of First Nation Market Culture," from *Aboriginal Policy Research*, volume 7, *A History of Treaties and Policies*, eds. Jerry P. White, Erik Anderson, Jean-Pierre Morin, and Dan Beavon (Toronto:

Thompson Educational Publishing, 2010), 118, http://thompsonbooks.com /wp-content/uploads/2020/02/APR_Vol_7Ch7.pdf.
26. Ann M. Carlos and Frank D. Lewis, *Commerce by a Frozen Sea: Native Americans and the European Fur Trade* (Philadelphia: University of Pennsylvania Press, 2010).
27. James P. Ronda, *Lewis and Clark among the Indians* (Lincoln: University of Nebraska Press, 1943), 75.
28. D. Bruce Johnsen, "The Potlatch as Fractional Reserve Banking," in *Unlocking the Wealth of Indian Nations*, ed. Terry L. Anderson (Washington, DC: Lexington Books, 2016).
29. Franz Boas, *Kwakiutl Ethnography*, ed. Helen Codere (Chicago: University of Chicago Press, 1966), 78.
30. Boas, 84–85.
31. Boas, 84–85.
32. Mann, *1491*, 370.
33. Hämäläinen, *Lakota America*, 16.
34. Hämäläinen, 17.
35. Hämäläinen, 17.
36. "Native American Money," Indians.org, accessed July 15, 2021, http://indians .org/articles/native-american-money.html.
37. "Native American Money."
38. Will Kenton, "Buck," Investopedia, updated Oct 27, 2020, https://www .investopedia.com/terms/b/buck.asp.

Chapter 2

1. "Southern Ute Indian Tribe: Living in La Plata County," Southern Ute Indian Tribe, Department of Natural Resources, accessed July 15, 2021, https://www .southernute-nsn.gov/natural-resources/lands/assignments/living-in-la-plata -county.
2. Richard K. Young, *The Ute Indians of Colorado in the Twentieth Century* (Norman: University of Oklahoma Press, 1997), 163.
3. "Southern Ute Indian Tribe."
4. Jonathan Thompson, "The Ute Paradox," *High Country News*, July 12, 2010, https://www.hcn.org/issues/42.12/the-ute-paradox.
5. Thompson, "Ute Paradox."
6. Private correspondence with Terry Anderson.
7. William C. Canby Jr., *American Indian Law in a Nutshell*, 6th ed. (St. Paul, MN: West Academic Publishing, 2015), 1–2.
8. Canby, 16.
9. Indian Land Tenure Foundation, "Issues: Land Tenure Issues," accessed July 15, 2021, https://iltf.org/land-issues/issues.

10. Stephen Cornell and Joseph Kalt, "Where's the Glue? Institutional and Cultural Foundations of American Indian Economic Development," *Journal of Socio-Economics* 29, no. 5 (2000): 443–70.
11. Canby, *American Indian Law*, 27.
12. Canby, 26–27.
13. Canby, 29–30.
14. Terry L. Anderson and Dominic P. Parker, "Sovereignty, Credible Commitments, and Economic Prosperity on American Indian Reservations," *Journal of Law and Economics* 51 (2008): 641–66.
15. "Grand Canyon Skywalk Judgment Could Devastate Tribe," *USA Today*, February 19, 2013.
16. Alison Berry, *Two Forests under the Big Sky: Tribal v. Federal Management*, PERC Policy Series no. 45 (Bozeman, MT: Property and Environment Research Center [PERC], 2009).
17. Matthew B. Krepps, "Can Tribes Manage Their Own Resources? The 638 Program and American Indian Forestry," in *What Can Tribes Do? Strategies and Institutions in American Indian Economic Development*, eds. Stephen Cornell and Joseph P. Kalt (Los Angeles: University of California, 1992), 179–203.
18. Berry, *Two Forests*, 17–18.
19. John Koppisch, "Why Are Indian Reservations So Poor? A Look at the Bottom 1%," *Forbes*, December 13, 2011.
20. Tulo Centre of Indigenous Economics, *Building a Competitive First Nation Investment Climate* (Kamloops, BC: Tulo Centre of Indigenous Economics, 2014), 48, https://www.tulo.ca/.
21. Shawn Regan and Terry L. Anderson, "Unlocking the Energy Wealth of Indian Nations," in *Unlocking the Wealth of Indian Nations*, ed. Terry L. Anderson (Washington, DC: Lexington Books, 2016).
22. Robert W. Middleton, Hearing before the Committee on Indian Affairs, US Senate. *Indian Energy Development: Statement of Dr. Robert W. Middleton*, 110th Congress, May 1, 2008.
23. Cornell and Kalt, "Where's the Glue?," 444.
24. Shawn Regan and Terry L. Anderson, "The Energy Wealth of Indian Nations," Property and Environment Research Center, 2013, http://perc.org/articles/energy-wealth-indian-nations.
25. Valerie Volcovici, "Red Tape Chokes Off Oil Drilling on Native American Reservations," Reuters, January 27, 2017, https://www.reuters.com/article/usa-trump-tribes-regulations/red-tape-chokes-off-drilling-on-native-american-reservations-idUSL1N1FH1BC.
26. Sierra Crane-Murdoch, "The Other Bakken Boom: A Tribe atop the Nation's Biggest Oil Play," Property and Environment Research Center (PERC) Case Study, November 28, 2012, https://www.perc.org/wp-content/uploads/old/pdfs/WEB-Bakken%20Case%20Study.pdf.

Chapter 3

1. New York: Crown Publishers, 2012.
2. Jasmine Simington and Nancy M. Pindus, "Mortgage Lending in Indian Country Has Jumped, but Land Policies Remain a Barrier," *Urban Wire* (blog), Urban Institute, April 20, 2017, https://www.urban.org/urban-wire/mortgage-lending-indian-country-has-jumped-land-policies-remain-barrier.
3. David Listokin, Kenneth Temkin, Nancy Pindus, David Stanek, and the Urban Institute, *Mortgage Lending on Tribal Land: A Report from the Assessment of American Indian, Alaska Native, and Native Hawaiian Housing Needs*, prepared for the US Department of Housing and Urban Development, Washington, DC, January 2017, https://www.huduser.gov/portal/publications/NAHSC-Lending.html.
4. Jennifer Birch, "Coalescence and Conflict in Iroquoian Ontario," *Archaeological Review* 25, no. 1 (2010): 29–48.
5. Barbara J. Williams and Maria del Carmen Jorge y Jorge, "Surface Area Computation in Ancient Mexico: Documentary Evidence of Acolhua-Aztec Proto-Geometry," *Symmetry: Culture and Science* 12, nos. 1–2 (2001): 185–200.
6. Lissa K. Wadewitz and Center for the Study of the Pacific Northwest, *The Nature of Borders: Salmon, Boundaries and Bandits on the Salish Sea* (Seattle: Center for the Study of the Pacific Northwest in association with University of Washington Press; Vancouver: UBC Press, 2012).
7. Michael Lebourdais, "Band Proposal Seeks to Regain Land Ownership, Restore Value," *Saskatoon StarPhoenix*, 2014, quoted in Tulo Centre of Indigenous Economics, *Building a Competitive First Nation Investment Climate* (Kamloops, BC: Tulo Centre of Indigenous Economics, 2014), https://www.tulo.ca/.
8. Pekka Hämäläinen, *Lakota American: A New History of Indigenous Power* (New Haven, CT: Yale University Press, 2019), 17.
9. Candy Moulton, "Chief Joseph's Guiding Principle," HistoryNet, originally published in *Wild West* (April 2014), https://www.historynet.com/chief-josephs-guiding-principle.htm.
10. Ovide Mercredi and Mary Ellen Turpel, *In the Rapids: Navigating the Future of First Nations* (Toronto: Viking, 1994), 70.
11. William C. Canby Jr., *American Indian Law in a Nutshell*, 6th ed. (St. Paul, MN: West Academic Publishing, 2015), 447.
12. Gavin Clarkson, "Tribal Finance and Economic Development—The Fight against Economic Leakage," in *American Indian Business: Principles and Practices*, eds. Deanna M. Kennedy, Charles F. Harrington, Amy Klemm Verbos, Daniel Stewart, Joseph Scott Gladstone, and Gavin Clarkson (Seattle: University of Washington Press, 2017), 68.

13. Terry L. Anderson and Dominic Parker, "Un-American Reservations," in *Defining Ideas* (Hoover Institution), February 24, 2011, https://www.hoover .org/research/un-american-reservations.

14. Canby, *American Indian Law*, 447.

15. For a discussion of how this has played out between the Navajo and the Hopi tribes, see Canby, *American Indian Law*, 447.

16. Indian Land Tenure Foundation, "Issues: Land Tenure Issues," accessed July 15, 2021, https://iltf.org/land-issues/issues.

17. Canby, *American Indian Law*, 449.

18. Indian Land Tenure Foundation, "Issues: Land Tenure Issues."

19. Indian Land Tenure Foundation, "Issues: Land Tenure Issues."

20. Canby, *American Indian Law*, 27.

21. Canby, 29.

22. "Eyes on the Future—While Holding On to Its Rich History, the Coushatta Tribe Is Focusing on Diversification, New Initiatives and Regional Outreach," *Greater Baton Rouge Business Report*, October 31, 2011.

23. Clarkson, "Tribal Finance and Economic Development," 83.

24. Hernando de Soto, *The Mystery of Capital: Why Capitalism Triumphs in the West and Fails Everywhere Else* (New York: Basic Books, 2000).

25. Clarkson, "Tribal Finance and Economic Development," 62.

26. US Department of the Interior, Bureau of Indian Affairs, "Indian Land Consolidation Program," accessed July 15, 2021.

27. US Department of the Interior, Land Buy-Back Program for Tribal Nations, "Landowners with Fractional Interests at the Santee Sioux Reservation Receive Buy-Back Program Offers," last edited May 15, 2019, https://www.doi.gov /buybackprogram/landowners-fractional-interests-santee-sioux-reservation -receive-buy-back-program.

Chapter 4

1. Charles C. Mann, *1491: New Revelations of the Americas before Columbus* (New York: Vintage Books, 2006), 292.

2. William C. Canby Jr., *American Indian Law in a Nutshell*, 6th ed. (St. Paul, MN: West Academic Publishing, 2015), 17.

3. Tucker Higgins and Dan Mangan, "Supreme Court Says Eastern Half of Oklahoma Is Native American Land," CNBC, July 9, 2020, https://www.cnbc .com/2020/07/09/supreme-court-says-eastern-half-of-oklahoma-is-native -american-land.html.

4. Stephen Cornell and Joseph Kalt, "Where's the Glue? Institutional and Cultural Foundations of American Indian Economic Development," *Journal of Socio-Economics* 29, no. 5 (2000): 443–70.

5. City of Sherrill, New York v. Oneida Indian Nation of New York et al., 544 U.S. 197 (2005).

6. Catherine Traywick, "A Tale of Two Tribes: Colorado's Southern Utes Want to Drill as Sioux Battle Pipeline," *Denver Post*, updated February 8, 2017, https://www.denverpost.com/2016/10/15/tribes-colorado-southern-utes-drill-sioux-battle-pipeline.

7. US Department of the Interior, Bureau of Indian Affairs, *Budget Justifications and Performance Information, Fiscal Year 2015*.

8. Kiowa Tribe of Okla. v. Manufacturing Technologies, Inc., 523 U.S. 751 (1998), https://supreme.justia.com/cases/federal/us/523/751.

9. Lawrence Hurley, "US Supreme Court Rejects Allergan Bid to Use Tribe to Shield Drug Patents," Reuters, April 15, 2019.

10. C & L Enterprises, Inc. v. Citizen Band Potawatomi Tribe of Oklahoma, 532 U.S. 411 (2001), https://supreme.justia.com/cases/federal/us/532/411.

11. National Conference of Commissioners on Uniform State Laws, Revised Model Tribal Secured Transactions Act (MTSTA), May 2017. For full text of MTSTA, see https://www.uniformlaws.org/HigherLogic/System/Download DocumentFile.ashx?DocumentFileKey = 2dc24255-67c3-2325-7a0e-58932 e3dc1bc.

12. Washington v. Confederated Tribes, 447 U.S. 134 (1980), 154–57.

13. White Mountain Apache Tribe v. State of Arizona, Department of Game & Fish, 649 F.2d 1274 (1981), https://law.justia.com/cases/federal/appellate-courts/F2/649/1274/459954.

14. *White Mountain Apache Tribe v. Arizona*.

15. Carole Goldberg, "Unraveling Public Law 280: Better Late Than Never," *Human Rights* (American Bar Association) 43, no. 1 (September 2017): 11.

16. Gavin Clarkson, "Tribal Finance and Economic Development—The Fight against Economic Leakage," in *American Indian Business: Principles and Practices*, eds. Deanna M. Kennedy, Charles F. Harrington, Amy Klemm Verbos, Daniel Stewart, Joseph Scott Gladstone, and Gavin Clarkson (Seattle: University of Washington Press, 2017), 102.

17. US Department of the Interior, Bureau of Indian Affairs, "Gaming Compacts," accessed July 15, 2021.

18. Gavin Clarkson and James Sebenius, "Leveraging Tribal Sovereignty for Economic Opportunity: A Strategic Negotiations Perspective," *Missouri Law Review* 76, no. 4 (2011), 1093–94.

19. Clarkson and Sebenius, "Leveraging Tribal Sovereignty," 1111.

20. Clarkson, "Tribal Finance and Economic Development," 83.

21. Clarkson, 84.

22. Clarkson, 84.

23. Becky Shay, "Crow Leader Outlines Plan for Fuel Plant," *Billings Gazette*, December 6, 2007.
24. Clarkson, "Tribal Finance and Economic Development," 84–85.
25. US Department of the Interior, Office of Indian Energy and Economic Development, "Why Tribes Should Adopt a Secured Transactions Code," *Tribal Economic Development Principles at a Glance Series*, April 8, 2019.
26. Native Nations Communications Task Force, "Improving and Increasing Broadband Deployment on Tribal Lands," report to the Federal Communications Commission from the Tribal Members of the Task Force, adopted November 5, 2019, 15, https://www.fcc.gov/sites/default/files/nnctf_tribal_broadband_report.pdf.
27. Native Nations Institute (University of Arizona), *Access to Capital and Credit in Native Communities* (Tucson: Native Nations Institute, 2016).
28. Indian Land Capital Company, "Lending," accessed July 15, 2021, https://www.ilcc.net/lending.
29. Ronald A. Wirtz. "Breaching the 'Buckskin' Curtain," *FedGazette* (Federal Reserve Bank of Minneapolis), September 1, 2000.
30. Office of the Comptroller of the Currency (United States), "Commercial Lending in Indian Country—Potential Opportunities in a Growing Market," February 2016, https://www.occ.gov/publications-and-resources/publications/community-affairs/community-developments-insights/ca-insights-feb-2016.html.

Chapter 5

1. Native Nations Institute (University of Arizona), *Access to Capital and Credit in Native Communities* (Tucson: Native Nations Institute, 2016), 10.
2. National Congress of American Indians (NCAI), "Tribal Infrastructure: Investing in Indian Country for a Stronger America," initial report to the Administration and Congress, 2017, 4, http://www.ncai.org/NCAI-InfrastructureReport-FINAL.pdf.
3. NCAI, "Tribal Infrastructure," 4.
4. Citizen Potawatomi Nation, Public Information Office, "Iron Horse Industrial Park Is on the Rails," Potawatomi.org, January 27, 2017, https://www.potawatomi.org/iron-horse-industrial-park-is-on-the-rails.
5. Catherine Sweeney, "The Citizen Potawatomi Nation Is Battling a Nationwide Problem with a Global Solution," *Journal Record* (Oklahoma City), January 31, 2018.
6. Frances Stead Sellers, "It's Almost 2020 and Almost 2 Million Americans Still Don't Have Running Water, According to New Report," *Washington Post*, December 19, 2019.
7. US Water Alliance, *Closing the Water Access Gap in the United States: A National Action Plan*, November 2019.

8. Sellers, "Almost 2 Million Americans."
9. NCAI, "Tribal Infrastructure," 3–4.
10. NCAI, 3–4.
11. NCAI, 6–8, 10–12, 17, 22.
12. Stephen Cornell and Miriam Jorgensen, "The Nature and Components of Economic Development in Indian Country," National Congress of American Indians Policy Research Center, May 2017, 13.
13. Cornell and Jorgensen, "Economic Development," 13.
14. Cornell and Jorgensen, 9.
15. Kaid Benfield, "A Native American Public Housing Project Returns to Its Roots," *City Lab* (Bloomberg), February 8, 2012, https://www.citylab.com /equity/2012/02/native-american-public-housing-project-returns-its-roots /1172.
16. Montana Budget and Policy Center, "Policy Basics: Taxes in Indian Country Part 2: Tribal Governments," November 2017, https://montanabudget.org /report/policy-basics-taxes-in-indian-country-part-2-tribal-governments.
17. Native Nations Institute, *Access to Capital*, 38.
18. Washington v. Confederated Tribes, 447 U.S. 134 (1980), 176.
19. Kelly S. Croman and Jonathan B. Taylor, "Why Beggar Thy Indian Neighbor? The Case for Tribal Primacy in Taxation in Indian Country," Joint Occasional Papers on Native Affairs (Tucson and Cambridge: Native Nations Institute and Harvard Project on American Indian Economic Development, 2016), 6, 8, https://nni.arizona.edu/publications-resources/publications/jopna/why -beggar-thy-indian-neighbor-case-tribal-primacy-taxation-indian-country.
20. NCAI, "Taxation," accessed April 20, 2020, http://www.ncai.org/policy-issues /tribal-governance/taxation.
21. Carl A. Calvert, "Part Three: Practical Applications to Construction Contracting in Indian Country," American Bar Association, 2005, 6, http://www.hardhatlaw .net/documents/2014/09/construction-on-tribal-lands.pdf.
22. Croman and Taylor, "Why Beggar Thy Indian Neighbor," 12.
23. Croman and Taylor, 10.
24. Croman and Taylor, 11.
25. Associated Press, "Oglala Sioux Tribe Approves Medical, Recreational Marijuana," March 11, 2020.
26. Croman and Taylor, "Why Beggar Thy Indian Neighbor," 16.
27. Jerry Cornfield, "Deal Ends Legal Fight and Allows Tulalips a Cut of Sales Tax," *Herald Business Journal* (Everett, WA), January 29, 2020.
28. Ron Ness, letter on behalf of Enerplus, Halcon Resources Corporation, Kodiak Oil & Gas Inc., Marathon Oil, Oasis Petroleum, Petro-Hunt, WPX Energy, QEP Resources Inc., and XTO to Senate Majority Leader R. Wardner, House Majority Leader A. Carlson, Senate Minority Leader M. Schneider,

House Minority Leader K. Onstad, Senator J. M. Warner, and Representative G. Froseth, February 15, 2013, quoted in Croman and Taylor, "Why Beggar Thy Indian Neighbor," 19; emphasis added by Croman and Taylor.

29. Croman and Taylor, "Why Beggar Thy Indian Neighbor," 21.
30. US Department of the Interior, Bureau of Indian Affairs (BIA), "Addressing the Harms of Dual Taxation in Indian Country through Modernizing the Indian Trader Regulations," February 15, 2017.
31. Native Nations Institute, *Access to Capital*, 80.
32. Native Nations Institute, 80.
33. Native Nations Institute, 86.
34. ChangeLab Solutions, "Shared Use Agreements & Tribal Nations," July 2015, 6, https://www.changelabsolutions.org/sites/default/files/SharedUse_TribalNations_FINAL_20150731.pdf.
35. Oneida Nation of Wisconsin, Service Agreement between Oneida Tribe of Indians of Wisconsin and Village of Ashwaubenon, January 8, 2014, https://oneida-nsn.gov/wp-content/uploads/2016/02/Service-Agreement-with-Ashwaubenon-2014.pdf.
36. BIA, "Financing a Tribal or Native-Owned Business," Tribal Economic Development Principles at a Glance Series, January 2016, 3.
37. Native Nations Institute, *Access to Capital*, 86.
38. Mark Fogarty, "Are Native CDFIs the Financial Institution of the Future?" *Indian Country Today*, September 1, 2017.
39. Native Nations Institute, *Access to Capital*, 17.
40. First Peoples Fund, "Rolling Rez Arts Is a New State-of-the-Art Mobile Arts Space," accessed April 25, 2020, https://www.firstpeoplesfund.org/rolling-rez-arts.
41. Cornell and Jorgensen, "Economic Development," 13–15.

Epilogue

1. Bill Yellowtail, "Indian Sovereignty: Dignity through Self-Sufficiency," *PERC Reports* 24, no. 2 (Summer 2006): 10–13.

BIBLIOGRAPHY

Acemoglu, Daron, Simon Johnson, and James A. Robinson. "Reversal of Fortune: Geography and Institutions in the Making of the Modern World Income Distribution." *Quarterly Journal of Economics* 117, no. 4 (November 2002): 1231–94.

Acemoglu, Daron, and James A. Robinson. *Why Nations Fail: The Origins of Power, Prosperity, and Poverty.* New York: Crown Publishers, 2012.

Anderson, Terry L. "Un-American Reservations." *Defining Ideas* (Hoover Institution), February 24, 2011.

Anderson, Terry L., ed. *Unlocking the Wealth of Indian Nations.* Washington DC: Lexington Books, 2016.

Anderson, Terry L., and Dominic P. Parker. "Sovereignty, Credible Commitments, and Economic Prosperity on American Indian Reservations." *Journal of Law and Economics* 51, no. 4 (November 2008): 641–66.

Anderson, Terry L., and Wilcomb E. Washburn. *Sovereign Nations or Reservations: An Economic History of American Indians.* San Francisco: Pacific Research Institute for Public Policy, 1995.

Associated Press. "Oglala Sioux Tribe Approves Medical, Recreational Marijuana." March 11, 2020.

Benfield, Kaid. "A Native American Public Housing Project Returns to Its Roots." *City Lab* (Bloomberg), February 8, 2012.

Berry, Alison. *Two Forests under the Big Sky: Tribal v. Federal Management.* PERC Policy Series no. 45. Bozeman, MT: Property and Environment Research Center (PERC), 2009.

Birch, Jennifer. "Coalescence and Conflict in Iroquoian Ontario." *Archaeological Review* 25, no. 1 (April 2010): 29–48.

Bleir, Garet, and Anya Zoledziowski. "Murdered and Missing Native American Women Challenge Police and Courts." Center for Public Integrity, updated October 29, 2018.

Boas, Franz. *Kwakiutl Ethnography*, edited by Helen Codere. Chicago: University of Chicago Press, 1966.

C & L Enterprises, Inc. v. Citizen Band Potawatomi Tribe of Oklahoma, 532 U.S. 411 (2001). https://supreme.justia.com/cases/federal/us/532/411.

Calvert, Carl A. "Part Three: Practical Applications to Construction Contracting in Indian Country." American Bar Association, 2005. http://www.hardhatlaw.net/documents/2014/09/construction-on-tribal-lands.pdf.

Canby, William C., Jr. *American Indian Law in a Nutshell*. 6th ed. St. Paul. MN: West Academic Publishing, 2015.

Carlos, Ann M., and Frank D. Lewis. *Commerce by a Frozen Sea: Native Americans and the European Fur Trade*. Philadelphia: University of Pennsylvania Press, 2010.

———. "The Economic History of the Fur Trade: 1670 to 1870." EH.net Encyclopedia, edited by Robert Whaples. March 16, 2008, https://eh.net/encyclopedia/the-economic-history-of-the-fur-trade-1670-to-1870.

ChangeLab Solutions. "Shared Use Agreements & Tribal Nations." July 2015. https://www.changelabsolutions.org/sites/default/files/SharedUse_Tribal Nations_FINAL_20150731.pdf.

Citizen Potawatomi Nation, Public Information Office. "Iron Horse Industrial Park Is on the Rails." Potawatomi.org, January 27, 2017. https://www.potawatomi.org/iron-horse-industrial-park-is-on-the-rails.

City of Sherrill, New York v. Oneida Indian Nation of New York et al., 544 U.S. 197 (2005). https://supreme.justia.com/cases/federal/us/544/197.

Clarkson, Gavin. "Tribal Finance and Economic Development: The Fight against Economic Leakage." In *American Indian Business: Principles and Practices*, edited by Deanna M. Kennedy, Charles F. Harrington, Amy Klemm Verbos, Daniel Stewart, Joseph Scott Gladstone, and Gavin Clarkson. Seattle: University of Washington Press, 2017.

Clarkson, Gavin, and James Sebenius. "Leveraging Tribal Sovereignty for Economic Opportunity: A Strategic Negotiations Perspective." *Missouri Law Review* 76, no. 4 (Fall 2011): 1093–94.

Colvin, George. "The Presence, Source and Use of Fossil Shark Teeth from Ohio Archaeological Sites." *Ohio Archaeologist* 61, no. 4 (Fall 2011).

Cornell, Stephen, and Miriam Jorgensen. "The Nature and Components of Economic Development in Indian Country." National Congress of American Indians Policy Research Center, May 2017.

Cornell, Stephen, and Joseph P. Kalt. "Where's the Glue? Institutional and Cultural Foundations of American Indian Economic Development." *Journal of Socio-Economics* 29, no. 5 (2000): 443–70.

Cornfield, Jerry. "Deal Ends Legal Fight and Allows Tulalips a Cut of Sales Tax" *Herald Business Journal* (Everett, WA), January 29, 2020.

Countries and Their Cultures. "Iroquois—Economy." Accessed July 15, 2021. https://www.everyculture.com/North-America/Iroquois-Economy.html.

Crane-Murdoch, Sierra. "The Other Bakken Boom: A Tribe atop the Nation's Biggest Oil Play." Property and Environment Research Center (PERC) Case Study. November 28, 2012. https://www.perc.org/wp-content/uploads/old/pdfs/WEB-Bakken%20Case%20Study.pdf.

Croman, Kelly S., and Jonathan B. Taylor. "Why Beggar Thy Indian Neighbor? The Case for Tribal Primacy in Taxation in Indian Country." Joint Occasional Papers on Native Affairs. Tucson and Cambridge: Native Nations Institute and Harvard Project on American Indian Economic Development, 2016.

Curtin, Sally C., and Holly Hedegaard. "Suicide Rates for Females and Males by Race and Ethnicity: United States, 1999 and 2017." Centers for Disease Control and Prevention, updated June 20, 2019.

De Soto, Hernando. *The Mystery of Capital: Why Capitalism Triumphs in the West and Fails Everywhere Else.* New York: Basic Books, 2000.

Economist Intelligence Unit. "Democracy Index 2019." https://www.eiu.com/topic/democracy-index/.

Ellis, Florence Hawley. "Isleta Pueblo." In *Handbook of North American Indians*, vol. 9. Washington, DC: Smithsonian Institution, 1979.

First Peoples Fund. "Rolling Rez Arts Is a New State-of-the-Art Mobile Arts Space." Accessed April 25, 2020. https://www.firstpeoplesfund.org/rolling-rez-arts.

Flanagan, Tom, Christopher Alcantara, and André Le Dressay. *Beyond the Indian Act: Restoring Aboriginal Property Rights.* Montreal: McGill-Queen's University Press, 2010.

Fogarty, Mark. "Are Native CDFIs the Financial Institution of the Future?" *Indian Country Today*, September 1, 2017.

Goldberg, Carole. "Unraveling Public Law 280: Better Late than Never." *Human Rights* (American Bar Association) 43, no. 1 (September 2017): 11.

Greater Baton Rouge Business Report. "Eyes on the Future—While Holding On to Its Rich History, the Coushatta Tribe Is Focusing on Diversification, New Initiatives and Regional Outreach." October 31, 2011.

Hamalainen, Pekka. *Lakota America: A New History of Indigenous Power.* New Haven, CT: Yale University Press, 2019.

Higgins, Tucker, and Dan Mangan. "Supreme Court Says Eastern Half of Oklahoma Is Native American Land." CNBC, July 9, 2020. https://www.cnbc

.com/2020/07/09/supreme-court-says-eastern-half-of-oklahoma-is-native-american-land.html.

Hudson's Bay Company. "History of HBC: Fur Trade." Accessed 2013. http://www.hbc.com/hbcheritage/history/business/fur/standardtrade.asp.

Hurley, Lawrence. "US Supreme Court Rejects Allergan Bid to Use Tribe to Shield Drug Patents." Reuters, April 15, 2019.

Indian Land Capital Company. "Lending." Accessed July 15, 2021. https://www.ilcc.net/lending.

Indian Land Tenure Foundation. "Issues: Land Tenure Issues." Accessed July 15, 2021. https://iltf.org/land-issues/issues.

Indians.org. "Native American Money." Accessed July 15, 2021. http://indians.org/articles/native-american-money.html.

Johnsen, D. Bruce. "The Potlatch as Fractional Reserve Banking." In *Unlocking the Wealth of Indian Nations*, edited by Terry L. Anderson. Washington DC: Lexington Books, 2016.

Kenton, Will. "Buck." Investopedia. Updated Oct 27, 2020. https://www.investopedia.com/terms/b/buck.asp.

Kiowa Tribe of Okla. v. Manufacturing Technologies, Inc., 523 U.S. 751 (1998). https://supreme.justia.com/cases/federal/us/523/751.

Koppisch, John. "Why Are Indian Reservations So Poor? A Look at the Bottom 1%." *Forbes*, December 13, 2011.

Krepps, Matthew B. "Can Tribes Manage Their Own Resources? The 638 Program and American Indian Forestry." In *What Can Tribes Do? Strategies and Institutions in American Indian Economic Development*, edited by Stephen Cornell and Joseph P. Kalt. Los Angeles: University of California, 1992.

Lear, Jonathan. *Radical Hope: Ethics in the Face of Cultural Devastation*. Cambridge: Harvard University Press, 2006.

Le Dressay, André, Normand Lavallee, and Jason Reeves. "First Nations Trade, Specialization, and Market Institutions: A Historical Survey of First Nation Market Culture." In *Aboriginal Policy Research*, volume 7, *A History of Treaties and Policies*, edited by Jerry P. White, Erik Anderson, Jean-Pierre Morin, and Dan Beavon. Toronto: Thompson Educational Publishing, 2010. http://thompsonbooks.com/wp-content/uploads/2020/02/APR_Vol_7Ch7.pdf.

Listokin, David, Kenneth Temkin, Nancy Pindus, David Stanek, and the Urban Institute. *Mortgage Lending on Tribal Land: A Report from the Assessment of American Indian, Alaska Native, and Native Hawaiian Housing Needs*. Prepared for the US Department of Housing and Urban Development,

Washington, DC, January 2017. https://www.huduser.gov/portal/publications/NAHSC-Lending.html.

Mann, Charles C. *1491: New Revelations of the Americas before Columbus*. New York: Vintage Books, 2006.

Mercredi, Ovide, and Mary Ellen Turpel. *In the Rapids: Navigating the Future of First Nations*. Toronto: Viking, 1994.

Middleton, Robert W. Hearing before the Committee on Indian Affairs, US Senate. *Indian Energy Development: Statement of Dr. Robert W. Middleton*, 110th Congress, Second Session, May 1, 2008.

Miller, Robert J. *Reservation "Capitalism": Economic Development in Indian Country*. Lincoln: University of Nebraska Press, 2013.

Montana Budget and Policy Center. "Policy Basics: Taxes in Indian Country Part 2: Tribal Governments." November 2017. https://montanabudget.org/report/policy-basics-taxes-in-indian-country-part-2-tribal-governments.

Moulton, Candy. "Chief Joseph's Guiding Principle." HistoryNet. Originally published in *Wild West* (April 2014). https://www.historynet.com/chief-josephs-guiding-principle.htm.

Muhammad, Dedrick Asante, Rogelio Tec, and Kathy Ramirez. "Racial Wealth Snapshot: American Indians / Native Americans." National Community Reinvestment Coalition, November 18, 2019.

National Congress of American Indians (NCAI). "Taxation." Accessed April 20, 2020. http://www.ncai.org/policy-issues/tribal-governance/taxation.

———. "Tribal Infrastructure: Investing in Indian Country for a Stronger America." NCAI to the Administration and Congress, 2017. http://www.ncai.org/NCAI-InfrastructureReport-FINAL.pdf.

National Conference of Commissioners on Uniform State Laws. Revised Model Tribal Secured Transactions Act, May 2017. https://www.uniformlaws.org/HigherLogic/System/DownloadDocumentFile.ashx?DocumentFileKey=2dc24255-67c3-2325-7a0e-58932e3dc1bc.

Native Nations Communications Task Force. "Improving and Increasing Broadband Deployment on Tribal Lands." Report to the Federal Communications Commission from the Tribal Members of the Task Force, adopted November 5, 2019. https://www.fcc.gov/sites/default/files/nnctf_tribal_broadband_report.pdf.

Native Nations Institute (University of Arizona). *Access to Capital and Credit in Native Communities*. Tucson: Native Nations Institute, 2016.

North, Douglass C. *Institutions, Institutional Change, and Economic Performance*. Cambridge: Cambridge University Press, 1990.

Office of the Comptroller of the Currency (United States). "Commercial Lending in Indian Country: Potential Opportunities in a Growing Market." February 2016. https://www.occ.gov/publications-and-resources/publications/community-affairs/community-developments-insights/ca-insights-feb-2016.html.

Oneida Nation of Wisconsin. "Service Agreement Between Oneida Tribe of Indians of Wisconsin and Village of Ashwaubenon." January 8, 2014. https://oneida-nsn.gov/wp-content/uploads/2016/02/Service-Agreement-with-Ashwaubenon-2014.pdf.

Perry, Ted. "Chief Seattle's Speech." Center for the Study of the Pacific Northwest, from film script for *Home* (Southern Baptist Radio and Television Commission, 1972). Reprinted in Rudolf Kaiser, "Chief Seattle's Speech(es): American Origins and European Reception," in *Recovering the Word: Essays on Native American Literature*, edited by Brian Swann and Arnold Krupat, 525–30. Berkeley: University of California Press, 1987.

Regan, Shawn, and Terry L. Anderson. "The Energy Wealth of Indian Nations." Property and Environment Research Center (PERC), 2013. http://perc.org/articles/energy-wealth-indian-nations.

———. "Unlocking the Energy Wealth of Indian Nations." In *Unlocking the Wealth of Indian Nations*, edited by Terry L. Anderson. Washington DC: Lexington Books, 2016.

Riley, Naomi Schaefer. *The New Trail of Tears: How Washington Is Destroying American Indians*. New York: Encounter Books, 2016.

Ronda, James P. *Lewis and Clark among the Indians*. Lincoln: University of Nebraska Press, 1943.

Sellers, Frances Stead. "It's Almost 2020 and Almost 2 Million Americans Still Don't Have Running Water, According to New Report." *Washington Post*, December 19, 2019.

Shay, Becky. "Crow Leader Outlines Plan for Fuel Plant." *Billings Gazette*, December 6, 2007.

Simington, Jasmine, and Nancy M. Pindus. "Mortgage Lending in Indian Country Has Jumped, but Land Policies Remain a Barrier." *Urban Wire* (blog), Urban Institute, April 20, 2017. https://www.urban.org/urban-wire/mortgage-lending-indian-country-has-jumped-land-policies-remain-barrier.

Smith, Adam. *An Inquiry into the Nature and Causes of the Wealth of Nations*, edited by Edwin A. Seligman. London: J. M. Dent, 1901.

Southern Ute Indian Tribe, Department of Natural Resources. "Southern Ute Indian Tribe: Living in La Plata County." Accessed July 15, 2021. https://www

.southernute-nsn.gov/natural-resources/lands/assignments/living-in-la-plata
-county.

Sweeney, Catherine. "The Citizen Potawatomi Nation Is Battling a Nationwide
Problem with a Global Solution." *Journal Record* (Oklahoma City), January 31,
2018.

Thompson, Johnathan. "The Ute Paradox." *High Country News*, July 12, 2010.

Traywick, Catherine. "A Tale of Two Tribes: Colorado's Southern Utes Want to
Drill as Sioux Battle Pipeline." *Denver Post*, updated February 8, 2017. https://
www.denverpost.com/2016/10/15/tribes-colorado-southern-utes-drill-sioux
-battle-pipeline.

Tulo Centre of Indigenous Economics. *Building a Competitive First Nation
Investment Climate*. Kamloops BC: Tulo Centre of Indigenous Economics,
2014. https://www.tulo.ca/.

UltimateWyoming.com. "Spanish Diggings." Accessed July 15, 2021. http://
ultimatewyoming.com/sectionpages/sec6/extras/spanishdiggings2.html.

US Department of the Interior, Bureau of Indian Affairs. "Addressing the Harms
of Dual Taxation in Indian Country through Modernizing the Indian Trader
Regulations." February 15, 2017.

———. *Budget Justifications and Performance Information, Fiscal Year 2015.*

———. "Financing a Tribal or Native-Owned Business." Tribal Economic Development Principles at a Glance Series, January 2016.

———. "Gaming Compacts." Accessed July 15, 2021.

———. "Indian Land Consolidation Program." Accessed July 15, 2021.

US Department of the Interior, Land Buy-Back Program for Tribal Nations.
"Landowners with Fractional Interests at the Santee Sioux Reservation Receive
Buy-Back Program Offers." Last edited May 15, 2019.

US Department of the Interior, Office of Indian Energy and Economic
Development. "Why Tribes Should Adopt a Secured Transactions Code."
Tribal Economic Development Principles at a Glance Series. April 8, 2019.

US Water Alliance. *Closing the Water Access Gap in the United States: A National
Action Plan*. November 2019.

USA Today. "Grand Canyon Skywalk Judgment Could Devastate Tribe."
February 19, 2013.

Volcovici, Valerie. "Red Tape Chokes Off Drilling on Native American
Reservations." Reuters, January 26, 2017. https://www.reuters.com/article/us
-usa-trump-tribes-regulations-insight/red-tape-chokes-off-drilling-on-native
-american-reservations-idUSKBN15B0E7.

Wadewitz, Lissa K., and Center for the Study of the Pacific Northwest. *The Nature of Borders: Salmon, Boundaries and Bandits on the Salish Sea*. Seattle: Center for the Study of the Pacific Northwest in association with University of Washington Press; Vancouver: UBC Press, 2012.

Washington v. Confederated Tribes, 447 U.S. 134 (1980). https://supreme.justia .com/cases/federal/us/447/134.

Western, Samuel. "Trade among Tribes: Commerce on the Plains before Europeans Arrived," WyoHistory.org (Wyoming State Historical Society), April 26, 2016. https://www.wyohistory.org/encyclopedia/trade-among-tribes-commerce -plains-europeans-arrived.

White Mountain Apache Tribe v. State of Arizona, Department of Game & Fish, 649 F.2d 1274 (1981). https://law.justia.com/cases/federal/appellate-courts/F2 /649/1274/459954.

Williams, Barbara J., and Maria del Carmen Jorge y Jorge. "Surface Area Computation in Ancient Mexico: Documentary Evidence of Acolhua-Aztec Proto-Geometry." *Symmetry: Culture and Science* 12, nos. 1–2, (2001): 185–200.

Williams, Judith. *Clam Gardens: Aboriginal Mariculture on Canada's West Coast*. Vancouver, BC: New Star Books, 2006.

Wilson, Paul S. "What Chief Seattle Said." *Environmental Law* 22, no. 4 (1992), 1457.

Wirtz, Ron. "Breaching the 'Buckskin Curtain.'" *FedGazette* (Federal Reserve Bank of Minneapolis), September 1, 2000.

Yellowtail, Bill. "Indian Sovereignty: Dignity through Self-Sufficiency." *PERC Reports* 24, no. 2 (Summer 2006): 10–13.

Young, Richard K. *The Ute Indians of Colorado in the Twentieth Century*. Norman: University of Oklahoma Press, 1997.

ABOUT THE AUTHORS

Terry L. Anderson is the John and Jean De Nault Senior Fellow at the Hoover Institution, Stanford University; past president of the Property and Environment Research Center, Bozeman, Montana; and professor emeritus at Montana State University. Much of his career has been focused on developing the ideas in his book *Free Market Environmentalism* (third edition, Palgrave Macmillan, 2015), cowritten with Donald R. Leal, outlining how markets and property rights can solve environmental problems. His most recent edited book on this theme is *Adapt and Be Adept: Market Response to Climate Change* (Hoover Institution Press, 2021). More recently Anderson has focused his research and writing on how Native American economies prior to European contact thrived based on property rights and markets, and how they were destroyed by federal dominance. Of his forty books, four have laid the foundation for his project Renewing Indigenous Economies (indigenousecon.org). The most recent of these books is *Unlocking the Wealth of Indian Nations* (Lexington Books, 2016). He lives in Montana with his wife, Monica, where they enjoy fishing, hunting, horseback riding, and skiing in Big Sky Country.

Kathy Ratté is a consultant in economics and online curriculum and instruction. Over twenty years teaching high school economics, civics, history, and composition in suburban Denver, Colorado,

Ratté earned both state and national awards in economics education and was selected to serve on the planning and writing committee for the National Assessment for Educational Progress in economics. She left public education in 2001 to become the curriculum development director and, subsequently, the director of online instruction for the nonprofit Foundation for Teaching Economics. In 2018, she joined the Alliance for Renewing Indigenous Economies as an educational consultant.

INDEX

ON THE COVER

Manny Jules, a former chief of the Kamloops Band (British Columbia, Canada) for sixteen years, is the artist who created *Alliance*, the cover artwork showing the North Star and the Southern Cross connected by two canoes. Not only does *Alliance* carry on the tradition of ledger art—a form of drawing on ledger paper that began in the late nineteenth century when Indians no longer had access to hides upon which to tell their stories—it depicts the connection of Indigenous people from both hemispheres. As Manny explains in his artist's statement at the front of the book, the Maori waka canoe and a North American Indian canoe, both paddled by several people, are symbols of the teamwork and determination that were an integral part of Indigenous history and are necessary today for renewing Indigenous economies.